THE KINGDOM KEEPERS

ALSO BY RIDLEY PEARSON

Cut and Run
The Body of David Hayes
The Art of Deception
Parallel Lies
Middle of Nowhere
The First Victim
The Pied Piper
Beyond Recognition
Chain of Evidence
No Witnesses
The Angel Maker
Hard Fall
Probable Cause
Undercurrents
Hidden Charges
Blood of the Albatross
Never Look Back

WITH DAVE BARRY

Peter and the Starcatchers

WRITING AS WENDELL McCALL

Dead Aim
Aim for the Heart
Concerto in Dead Flat

WRITING AS JOYCE REARDON

The Diary of Ellen Rimbauer: My Life as Rose Red

THE KINGDOM KEEPERS

FROM THE COAUTHOR OF *PETER AND THE STARCATCHERS*

RIDLEY PEARSON

EDITIONS

New York

Printed in the United States of America
First Edition
10 9 8 7 6 5 4 3 2
Library of Congress Cataloging-in-Publication Data on file.
ISBN: 0-7868-5444-8

*This book is dedicated to anyone and everyone who ever wondered what happens when the gates are closed and the **lights go out**.*

ACKNOWLEDGMENTS

To whoever invented holograms, thanks for the ride.

Without people who make books come true, like Al Zuckerman and Amy Berkower at Writers House, and Wendy Lefkon, my editor at Disney Editions, projects like this would never happen. Thanks to you all.

Thanks also to Laurel and David, who read this far too many times, red pens in hand. And to Christopher Caines for his keen eye and great suggestions.

And thanks to Jason Surrell, a Disney Imagineer who has the "keys to the kingdom." He toured me through an empty Magic Kingdom on more than one occasion, and helped to make magic out of reality. Jason repeatedly served up the history of and little-known facts about the park, though he'll probably deny it in order to keep his job.

Thanks, too, to Wayne and Christina—and a dozen more who shall remain nameless—who live this fiction. Wayne works behind the scenes at Splash Mountain, and the lovely Christina at Space Mountain. They provided mountains of help.

Special thanks to Paige, Storey, and Sophie, through whose eyes I've seen the Magic Kingdom so many times now, and who got me wondering what it must be like at night after everyone's departed . . . or *almost* everyone.

And thanks to Dave, who teased me relentlessly for my study of the trash evacuation system during one of our secret tours of the tunnels. This is for you. There really *is* method to this madness. Or sort of.

—*R.P.*
February 28, 2005
St. Louis, Missouri

He found himself standing next to the flagpole in Town Square, in the heart of the Magic Kingdom. In his pajamas. How he'd gotten here, he had no idea. His last memory was climbing into bed—it felt like only minutes earlier.

Gripped by a sense of panic, awed by the sight of the Cinderella Castle at night, Finn Whitman briefly recalled that he'd had other, similar dreams recently—always in the Magic Kingdom, always at night. But in his thirteen years, none so real, so vivid as this: he felt a breeze on his face; he smelled the wet earth of a flower bed not far away; he heard the distant whine of traffic and the buzz of a motorboat on the lake behind him.

"It looks so different," he thought, only to realize he'd spoken out loud. Main Street stood empty, not a person in sight. He glanced around and quickly saw that he was all alone.

"Not so different as all that," came a man's voice. Though faint, it startled Finn. He looked around again, this time trying to find the source of that voice.

There! An old guy with white hair, on a bench in

front of the Exhibition Hall. He sat so close to a seated sculpture of Goofy that Finn hadn't noticed him.

Finn moved toward the man, crossing the empty street. He felt unusually light, almost buoyant.

The old man wore khakis, a collared shirt, and a name tag: WAYNE.

"Where is everybody?" Finn asked, struck by the electronic sound of his own voice.

"Is it empty?" the man asked, looking up anxiously. "Tell me what you see."

Finn wondered if the old guy was blind. He seemed to be looking right at Finn; his blue eyes looked perfectly normal. Still, maybe he couldn't see.

"Well," Finn said politely, "it's like . . . empty. And it's dark out. And it's just the two of us."

Wayne's expression changed to disappointment.

"What am I supposed to see, exactly?" Finn asked.

"You're only supposed to see what you can see."

"Whatever that means," Finn said.

"It means exactly what it says."

"If you say so."

"Listen, young man, I've been around here since long before any of them were even created. I live in the apartment above the fire station." He pointed right at the firehouse and then looked back at Finn. "That takes some seniority, believe me."

Seniority or senility? Finn wondered. Living above the firehouse? Finn doubted it.

"Nice pajamas," the old guy said.

Finn looked at himself. His pajamas seemed to be . . . glowing. What was with that? He said, "I don't mean to be rude, but if you can see, if you're not blind, then why'd you ask me about the park being empty?"

Wayne's ice-blue eyes drilled into him. "How do you think you got here, young man?"

"That depends on where I am," Finn answered honestly. This felt like no dream he'd ever experienced.

"Very good answer. I expected no less of you."

"Excuse me?"

"I assumed that you'd question this—that's only natural—but ultimately there's only one explanation, isn't there?"

"Is there?" Finn asked, confused.

"The other ones I wasn't so sure about. But you, Finn Whitman. By the way, that's a fine name you have. A name with real potential."

Finn took a step back. How did this old guy know his name?

"What other ones?" Finn asked. He studied Town Square and Main Street. The street lamps shone yellow. The Cinderella Castle glowed in the distance. All the familiar streets and paths and attractions, but empty.

"I told you, there's no one here. No one but us. It's empty."

Wayne said nothing as he stood and walked up Main Street, past the shops and toward the castle. Finn found himself following right along. They reached Central Plaza, an island in the center of a traffic circle, the spokes of which led to the Magic Kingdom's various lands—Tomorrowland, Frontierland, Liberty Square. They stopped in front of a statue of Walt Disney with Mickey Mouse. The castle rose majestically into the night sky.

"What time is it?" Wayne asked.

As Finn brought his arm up to look at his watch, he saw that his arm wasn't exactly his arm. It was . . . glowing. Not only glowing, but he could almost see through it. As if—

"What's going on?" Finn asked. "What's with my arm?"

Wayne sounded critical as he said, "Figure it out." He then reached into his pocket and removed what looked like a remote control for a car: a small black plastic fob with a single red button. It looked like a garage-door opener.

"What's with that thing?" Finn asked.

"This button will send you back."

"Back where?" Finn felt a jolt of fear. What if this

wasn't a dream? He studied his arm again. Then his other arm. He looked down at his legs. His whole body was glowing and vaguely translucent.

"Back to bed," Wayne answered.

"So it is a dream? I thought so."

"It's not a dream."

Finn saw a pair of four-foot-tall chipmunks come out of the castle. They walked down a path and turned left, toward Toontown. He felt himself staring. He recognized them.

"What?" Wayne asked excitedly.

"Nothing," Finn answered.

"You saw something!" he practically shouted into Finn's ear, causing Finn to jump back, startled.

Wayne leaped up, suddenly years younger. He pulled Finn to his feet.

"You saw something!" he thundered.

"Hey! What's the big deal?"

"Tell me what you saw."

"You saw it too!" Finn told him.

"Which character?"

Finn felt relief. Wayne knew Finn had seen a character, which had to mean he'd seen it too. He was clearly playing some kind of game, making Finn actually name the character, but Finn was good at games.

"Which character did you see?" Finn asked.

"You want me to push this button?" Wayne threatened.

Did he? Finn wasn't sure. If it was a dream, the black remote-control fob represented a way out. When was the right time to use it? He hoped to stretch this out a minute longer. It was fun here.

He glanced around at the sound of footsteps. Goofy went tearing past them, not thirty feet away, and headed into Frontierland.

Wayne never moved. Never looked in Goofy's direction.

"You're playing head games with me," Finn said.

"Am I?"

"Goofy," Finn said.

"Are you asking me if I'm goofy? I've been called worse." Wayne studied Finn. His old leathery face brightened as he said, "You saw Goofy!"

Maybe Wayne needed a hearing aid—he seemed prone to fits of shouting.

Finn backed off. "Yeah. So what? You would have too, if you'd bothered to look."

Wayne probably couldn't hear all that well. He obviously hadn't heard Goofy's footsteps, because he hadn't turned toward the sound.

Finn decided to test Wayne. "Chip and Dale," he said. "You saw them, right?"

"You saw Chip and Dale?" He made it sound like Finn had won the lottery. What was with that?

"I, ah . . . This is getting a little weird. I think I want to go back now." Finn heard himself repeat some of what Wayne had told him, though the words didn't fit in his mouth all that well. It sounded to him like someone else doing the talking.

"I'll push the button, if you like. But I have to warn you. . . ." Wayne fiddled with the nametag pinned to his uniform.

"Warn me about what?"

"What you'll be missing. The park after dark. Basically all to yourself. The attractions operate day and night. Not many people know that."

"Now I know I'm dreaming."

"But you aren't," Wayne explained. "Are you forgetting your arm?"

Finn studied his arm once more. "I'll admit, that is . . . interesting. It's almost like—" Finn caught himself.

"Like you're glowing," Wayne said in an all-knowing, I-told-you-so tone of voice.

"Am I?"

"What might account for that?" Wayne inquired.

Finn understood somehow that a lot hung on his answer—his imagining this place, or dreaming it, or whatever was happening to him. His ability to stay here.

To return. He wasn't quick to answer. He didn't want to face what Wayne was suggesting.

"I give up," he said.

"No, you don't," Wayne protested. "You never would have been chosen for this if you were the kind who gives up on things. You're a finisher, Finn. That's what I liked about you from your first audition tape."

Stunned by what the old guy had just said, Finn felt his mouth go dry. How did Wayne know about his audition tape? Exactly how complicated could a dream get?

"Who are you?" Finn blurted out.

"I'm Wayne. I work here. I was one of the first people hired by Walt Disney to imagine this park. The rides, the attractions. They call us Imagineers."

"You knew Walt Disney?" Finn tried not to sound impressed.

"He was my boss, you might say. At any rate, he's the reason I'm here. The reason you're here."

"Me?"

"I know this can't be easy."

"It's a dream," Finn said, thinking, What's so hard about a dream?

"No, it's not a dream," Wayne said. "Take a look at the moon." Finn didn't move. Wayne's voice became more severe. "I said: look at the moon."

Finn had to turn around to locate the moon. A half-moon, like a crooked smile, hung well above the horizon.

"When you wake up—when you think you wake up—take a look out the window. You'll see the same moon, and you'll know."

"Know what?" Finn asked.

"That you were here. Sitting here in Disney World with an old guy named Wayne."

"You're telling me this isn't a dream?" Finn felt his words catch in his throat.

"We've got a problem. A big problem. A problem that affects not only the park, but the world outside the park. We call them the Overtakers."

"The what?" Finn didn't like the sound of that.

Wayne said urgently, "You need to contact the other hosts. All four. Arrange to meet them here at the same time. That will mean all of you going to bed, going to sleep, fairly close to the same time. Within a half hour of one another. Tell them that. That should work, I think."

"What are you talking about?"

"There's a fable, a story, a puzzle of sorts that was left in case of a problem like this. It's called the Stonecutter's Quill."

"A problem like what?" Finn felt totally confused. The Stonecutter's Quill—the title had an eerie sound.

Just then, Tom Sawyer came out of Frontierland and

headed up a long ramp into the castle. Is that really *the* Tom Sawyer? Finn wondered. The barefoot boy was smoking a pipe with a long stem. Wayne did a good job of not reacting, of pretending he didn't see the kid.

Wayne said, "The puzzle has to be solved to be understood. It has to be understood to be of any use to us." He paused and looked over at Finn. It felt to Finn as if Wayne were looking right through him. "You're going to solve it."

"Me?"

"The five of you," Wayne said.

Finn jumped away from the man. Again he thought: how complicated can a dream get? If Wayne was only a part of the dream, how could he possibly know about the four other hosts? How could he talk about Finn's audition tape the way he had? It was all related, all rolled into one, but Finn couldn't sort it out.

Finn said, "You're talking about MGM Studios."

"Of course I am," Wayne said. "You see? I knew you were the right one. You're the leader, Finn."

"I don't have the slightest clue what you're talking about," Finn said.

"Nice try. But of course you do. You know exactly what I'm talking about. You just don't want to face it. Perfectly understandable. That will change."

"A fable," Finn said, testing him again. Could a dream remember itself?

"The moon," Wayne reminded him. "Don't forget the moon."

"I won't."

"All five of you. I need you together. Here. All in the same place at the same time. I can explain it to you then. Once. As a group. Just the one time. You can decide—as a group—to help us or not."

"Us?" Finn said.

"I'll explain that as well."

"This is the weirdest dream I've ever had!" Finn said, not realizing he was shouting.

"You'll get over it," Wayne said. He raised his right hand—the one carrying the black remote-control fob—and pressed the button with his thumb.

Finn awoke, sitting up in bed. His bedside clock read 2:07 A.M. He collected himself, checked his surroundings. He reached out and touched the glass of water next to the clock. Just the feel of it was reassuring. Thank goodness, he thought.

A dream? he wondered. "Whoa," he heard himself say aloud. "What a dream!" This time his voice sounded more the way it always sounded, which reminded him of how thin and electronic it had sounded in the park.

"Whoa," he repeated, just to hear himself say it. He scratched an itch on his head, and another on his belly. That felt better. He lay back down, his head on the pillow, his green eyes wide open to the dark room.

All at once Finn spotted a shaft of light—bluish light—on his ceiling. It was in the shape of a knife blade. *Moonlight.*

Finn slipped out of bed with trepidation. He crept toward the window, afraid to look. The closer he got to it, the more his face was bathed in that pale light seeping through a small crack in the curtains.

Finn raised his arm and caught sight of his watch. His arm appeared *solid*. It did not glow and shimmer the way it had while he was with Wayne. That came as a relief.

Finn parted the curtains.

There, out the window, hanging *in the exact same place* in the sky, where Wayne had pointed it out to him, Finn saw the curving smile of a half-moon. Could he have known that in his sleep? How? He looked again.

The moon seemed to be laughing at him.

The hallways of Finn's middle school could sometimes feel as long as runways. Late for class, he found this to be one of those times. Steel lockers occupied most of the space between the doors to the classrooms. The lockers were covered with stickers and pictures of movie stars or pro athletes, which instantly distinguished a girl's locker from a boy's. Fluorescent-tube lighting cast a sickly glow over everything, and made human skin look vaguely greenish.

"He said there was a fable. A story of some kind," Finn said to the boy standing next to him. "That my friends and I are supposed to save the park, or something." He realized how ridiculous this sounded. "Whatever that means."

"By 'friends' you mean like, me?" Dillard Cole asked. Dillard ate enough for two kids and had the body to show for it.

"He didn't mean you, Dillard," Finn said gently, trying not to hurt the guy's feelings. "Not exactly. He meant the other . . . the hosts. At Disney World. The DHIs."

"No way."

"Way," Finn said, hurrying off to his fourth-period classroom.

"It was only a dream!" Dillard shouted after him.

Finn wasn't so sure about that.

"We're honored you could join us, Mr. Whitman," said Mr. Richardson as Finn rushed in to his world history class. Mr. Richardson was probably the most boring teacher in the entire school. He'd lived in the U.S. for twenty-some years, but still spoke with a thick British accent. He sounded like a pompous snob.

Finn checked the wall clock; he was eight minutes late, just under the ten-minute deadline when Richardson would have given him a tardy. Three tardies meant after-school study hall. Finn already had collected two others, both from science class.

"You'll sit up front, please," Mr. Richardson said, indicating an empty chair. Torture on top of humiliation. "For the record, your notoriety pulls no weight in my class. I beg you to remember that when grades are issued. I find the idea of child actors tedious at best."

"Sorry I'm late," Finn said, sliding down into the chair, resentful that he'd been made to apologize.

He'd taken the job at Disney World somewhat against his will, mostly at his mother's urging. At the time she'd had no idea she was making him into a middle-school rock star. He remembered it well.

"There will be money in it," his mother had said. "Your father and I can put a little something away for your college."

"I don't know, Mom," Finn had complained.

"This is Walt Disney World, don't forget. You would be a host, like a guide, in Walt Disney World."

"It's not exactly *me*."

"It'll look like you. Sound like you. It'll seem like you to everyone but you. You'd be there for years, Finn Whitman. Maybe forever. You can't get any 'cooler' than Disney World."

His mother didn't know everything, but when she was right she was right. Finn loved the Disney parks. So did his friends. Even though they lived in Orlando, they all went to the parks whenever they could afford it. "But the Magic Kingdom, Mom? It's for little kids. At Disney-MGM, sure! Animal Kingdom would be awesome. But the Magic Kingdom?"

"You love the Magic Kingdom, and you know it. Besides, the rest of your family would get complimentary passes—several a year, every year, for life. As in, forever. We could basically go whenever we want."

"Without me."

"I thought you just said you're too old for the Magic Kingdom." Finn's mom could twist almost anything he said. He picked his arguments carefully with her. She had explained the terms of the contract to him, but Finn hadn't really paid attention.

"Tell me about the disguise stuff again," he said.

"You would only be allowed to visit the Magic Kingdom with prior approval. Once permission is granted, you'd still have to go in disguise. But a hat and sunglasses would be enough. You'd only have to wear them when you're in the Magic Kingdom. They can't have two of you running around, the real you and the hologram-host you. It makes sense if you think about it."

It did make sense, but he wasn't about to admit that.

She said, "It sounds so easy. All you do is let them film you walking and gesturing. You read the script a couple times into a microphone. They process the film, or whatever, and, presto! You're a hologram-host at the Magic Kingdom. With a college nest egg and lifetime complimentary passes. Finn, you love special effects! What they're offering is for you to *be* the special effect. How much cooler can that be?" She was right again, but he resisted an all-out agreement. His mother had once called a new toaster "high-tech." What did she know?

"All I have to do is audition?" he asked, testing her.

"That's right! They might not even take you."

"Mom," Finn said, "this is me we're talking about. Of course they'll take me."

"Excuse me, Mr. Hotshot, but I do not want to hear you talking that way, and you know it. If this is going to go to your head, we are not doing this."

Actually, Finn's mom loved to hear him talk that way, though she pretended otherwise. She had schooled him in self-confidence. He'd auditioned for several things and never won a part yet, but not because he lacked confidence.

"Okay. I'll do it," he said.

She beamed. He loved to see her like that—bright-eyed and childlike.

A month after Finn had passed the final audition and won a place as a Disney Host Interactive, or DHI, he arrived at an enormous soundstage at Disney-MGM Studios.

The size of a jet aircraft hangar, the soundstage was rigged with hundreds of film lights, a green screen that filled one entire wall, trampolines, cameras, boom microphones, and dozens of scruffily dressed crew members. He'd never seen anything like it, except in movies, though he did his best to pretend otherwise. A college-age girl dressed in black and gray wore a headset with a microphone mouthpiece, a fuzzy black ball by her lips. She called herself a "PA." It took Finn four days to realize that that stood for *production assistant.*

Her boss was a guy named Brad, from Disney Imagineering.

Brad made Finn dress in green tights and a green stretchy top and walk around on a green stage. The costume had small metal sensors, like thin coins, stuck to the tights on every joint of his body—dozens of the things. Cameras hooked up to a computer recorded the movement of the small metal disks. In the cameras' eyes, the green costume, moving against the green background, basically made Finn's body disappear. The computer saw him instead as a floating cloud of shiny points. The engineers would later use the recordings of Finn's movements to animate the holograms of Finn and the other kids. Brad explained that this process was called "motion capture."

There were five kids in all. One very pretty girl, Charlene, had sandy blond hair and blue eyes, with pale skin. The other girl, Willa, struck him as a little geeky, but extremely smart. She was sweet, but not knockout gorgeous like Charlene. Not many girls looked like Charlene. Willa struck him as moody. With her hooded brown eyes and dark, braided hair, she might have been Asian or Native American. Maybeck, an African American kid, was taller than Finn by a full head and had the big-guy attitude to go along with it. For some reason he made a point of telling Finn that he was a Baptist. Finn, who wasn't terribly religious, wasn't sure what to do with that information, nor even what it meant.

On a break, Finn hung out with Maybeck and the last of the five, a boy who introduced himself as Philby. Like Maybeck, he obviously preferred to be called by his last name.

Philby looked older than all of them, but was in fact the same age. He had a British accent or something close to it—Australia or New Zealand, Finn guessed.

"Quite the motley group," Philby said.

"We're the Orlando assortment pack," Maybeck quipped. "One of every flavor."

Finn said, "We're all from different schools, right? What's with that? It's like they wanted to make sure none of us knew each other. Why would they do that?"

"Control," Maybeck answered. "These kinds of guys . . . with them it's all about control. That guy, Brad? I don't trust him. He's keeping stuff from us. Count on it."

Finn liked Brad, but he knew what Maybeck was talking about. It did feel like they weren't being told everything.

"We'd better be able to trust him," Finn suggested. "He's the one turning us into holograms."

"I don't know about you," Maybeck answered, "but I never trust anyone but myself." He added a little late, "No offense."

Finn wanted out of his tights.

Philby said, "Did you know that DHI—Disney Host Interactive—also stands for Daylight Hologram Imaging?"

"Seriously?" Finn asked.

"Totally."

"See?" Maybeck said. "That's what I'm talking about—right there. First I've heard of it."

Philby continued, "This has never been done before. DHIs. Not like this. We're going to be turned into absolutely perfect three-dimensional images. Duplicates of ourselves. We'll look real, but we'll be made of nothing but light. It's pretty cool technology, actually."

"But if it's never been done before," Finn said, "how do we know it's safe?"

The boys glanced back and forth between themselves. Philby said, "It's like taking pictures, that's all. How can it not be safe?"

"It pays," Maybeck said harshly. "That's all I care about. My aunt could use the extra money."

"Your aunt?" Finn said, before he took the time to think that his question might sound rude.

"Yeah," Maybeck said. "I live with my aunt. My parents . . . They aren't around."

Finn felt awful for having asked. Maybeck grew

silent. He seemed less tough all of a sudden.

"Sorry," Finn said, "for asking."

"Not your problem," Maybeck said in a softer voice. "My aunt's cool. She tried to get me in a toothpaste ad, but I lost out. Then this thing came up. Brad told me that if I'd gotten that ad I'd never have been asked to be a host. They want nothing but fresh faces."

"So you got lucky," Finn said.

"We all got lucky," Maybeck agreed. "A DHI in the Magic Kingdom? We're going to be famous."

"We're going to be ghosts," Philby corrected. "Electronic ghosts, provided that this technology actually works."

"Don't say stuff like that," Maybeck pleaded. "Of course it works."

"Of course," Philby said. "My bad." But he sounded less than convinced.

3

"I don't get it," Dillard said as he gripped Finn's ankles for sit-ups. There were about forty kids on the crabgrass doing various forms of exercise out behind the school, in a field enclosed by a corroded chain-link fence. The South Florida climate ate metal down to rust and turned wood to sponge. Only concrete had a fighting chance. The kids, spread around the field in clumps, tried to make it look like they were exercising. Dirt stuck to Finn's arms and the back of his neck. He looked up at the ocean-blue sky full of billowing white clouds.

"The other DHIs," Finn explained. "The Disney Hosts . . . I've got to hook up with them before I go back."

"You know how stupid that sounds?"

"Yeah, but I don't care. No matter what, I've got to find out if they've had similar . . . dreams."

Dillard glanced up and immediately let go of Finn's ankles. Finn went head over heels backward. He found himself looking at an upside-down version of a girl named Amanda Lockhart, who had transferred to the school in late September, a few weeks earlier. She had exotic-looking eyes, a deep, natural tan, and a few freckles on her cheeks. She was stretching along with a dozen other girls. Finn wasn't big on girls, but something about Amanda grabbed and held his attention.

Dillard clasped his ankles again. Finn struggled back up to sitting.

He squeezed out a couple more sit-ups. "It's *experimental*," he explained. "The DHI technology. Not exactly photography, not exactly computer graphics."

"You're going psycho on me," Dillard complained.

Finn said, "When I woke up, the moon was right where it belonged. You want to explain that?"

"I'm sorry to have to tell you this," Dillard said, "but I think they fried your brain."

"I don't know any of their full names. Willa, Charlene, Maybeck, and Philby. Maybeck and Philby will be easier to find than the girls, because those are their last names, unusual names at that. There was this guy at MGM who ran things. He would know who everyone is, though I'm not sure he'd tell me."

Dillard gave Finn a puzzled look. "I feel sorry for you, man. You've lost it."

"The new girl: Amanda. Doesn't her mother or father work over at MGM? Did you hear about that?"

Many of the students' parents had something to do with one of the parks.

"Amanda is a *girl*," Dillard reminded Finn. "Have you lost your mind?" Dillard thought of girls as a separate life-form.

"Yeah," Finn said. "Maybe I have."

The monorail zoomed past a sea of green trees, heading for a stop at the Grand Floridian Hotel. "This is pretty cool of you, Amanda," Finn said. He wore a Tampa Devil Rays baseball cap and a pair of his father's old sunglasses, which looked too big for his face. Some disguise. Amanda wore hip huggers and a shirt that exposed her belly button.

"We're taking photographs?" she asked.

"They're friends of mine, you see?"

"Sort of." Then she confessed, "No, not really."

"I don't know their full names, so I don't know how to find them. If I can get photographs of their DHIs and show them around some of the other schools, then maybe someone will recognize them. I'm not sure what else to do."

"Word is, you're going psycho," Amanda said. "I wasn't about to get you mad at me."

"I'm not stabbing girls in showers or anything."

"That's a relief." Amanda allowed a hint of a smile that Finn knew she would rather not have revealed. It wasn't cool for a girl to show she liked a boy any more

25

than the opposite. Boys and girls seemed to spend a lot of time and energy trying to convince one another that they didn't exist.

Finn explained, "The problem is, if I'm going to visit the Magic Kingdom, my admission has to be pre-approved. That means telling my parents, and I can't exactly explain this to them."

"You haven't exactly explained it to me. Listen, I don't mind using a couple of my family's comp tickets, Finn. If you're worried you owe me, you don't."

"Cool."

"Is everything *cool* to you?" she asked. "What's with you and that word?"

"You're cool," he said, looking right at her. Where did that come from?

She blushed and bit her lower lip to keep from grinning. She looked out the monorail car's window, as if she hadn't seen the Grand Floridian a hundred times.

"So why'd you agree to help me, anyway?" he asked, coaxing her. The doors hissed shut. A recorded voice announced that the next stop was the Magic Kingdom.

She glanced out the window too. "Because . . . I have my reasons. I want to help." She spoke to the glass. Then she looked directly at Finn and said, "Besides, I've never met a real psycho before."

"Very funny."

"I thought so."

When she laughed, it reminded him of bells. He made a mental note not to tell Dillard that.

At the entrance to the Magic Kingdom, Amanda handled the complimentary tickets while Finn kept his head down so as not to be recognized. A minute later they were inside the main gate, passing the spot where parents picked up and returned the rented baby strollers.

Still looking at the pavement, Finn asked her, "Do you see any obvious security types?"

"No."

"They don't all wear uniforms. They're pretty hard to spot."

"Finn, you're not exactly one of the ten most wanted, or something. We're going to be fine. Hey! There's a host over there," Amanda said. "It's not you," she announced.

Finn looked over. A crowd had gathered around the DHI. "That's Charlene," he said.

"You ready?"

"Yes."

"Okay, then. Here goes."

Amanda slinked over toward the crowd, then posed for a shot with Charlene as Finn raised his father's

digital camera. Charlene looked perfectly real—
absolutely real—until a kid walked through her. The
DHI never stopped talking, never noticed that a kid was
playing with her.

"You've gone awfully quiet," Amanda said a
moment later, as she rejoined Finn.

"I'd never seen that before. A kid walking through
a DHI like that."

"They shouldn't be allowed to do that," Amanda
said. "It's disrespectful."

It wasn't the actual act that bothered Finn. It was
the concept. A hologram was nothing but light—
a three-dimensional image. How could he become one
by falling asleep? What was he thinking?

"Do you believe in weird stuff?" Finn asked her.

"Depends how weird, I suppose."

"Real weird."

"Try me."

But at that moment Amanda spotted another DHI
and started toward it.

Maybeck.

Finn's legs didn't move. He felt something odd.
Like someone was watching him. He spun around.

Main Street was crowded with people. Finn
searched faces, his focus shifting.

He stopped on a white-haired guy—an old guy—

wearing a barbershop costume that made him look even older. Wayne! He was looking right at Finn, the same way Finn's dad looked at him when Finn had done something wrong.

Wayne signaled for Finn to look to his left.

There, Finn saw four older guys in band uniforms—red jackets with brass buttons. It took him a second to realize they were headed right for him.

Security?

Finn turned to Amanda, who was posing with Maybeck, expecting Finn to shoot a picture. He called out to her, "Trouble!"

They'd discussed this possibility and reviewed various options. They had agreed that if they had to separate for any reason, they would try to meet up again at the exit from the Haunted Mansion. Amanda took off at a run without a second thought. Finn tucked his father's camera into his pocket and ducked into the Emporium. Made to look like an old-time general store, it sold everything Disney—clothing, dolls, stuffed animals, CDs, and DVDs. It was packed wall-to-wall with shoppers.

Finn hurried past several displays, deeper into the store. He passed shelves of princess costumes. A rack of hats and caps. A poster hung from the ceiling by a string, announcing the Virtual Magic Kingdom. He stopped and used a mirror to watch the store windows behind him. There he saw a uniformed band musician enter the store.

Coincidence? The band musician glanced to his right. Finn followed that line of sight—to another band member. They exchanged a look, and then they turned and scanned the store.

Finn felt sick with fear. He'd blown it, entering the park without the proper authorization. His family would probably lose their comp tickets. He supposed his DHI might even be terminated. They were coming for him: quickly, and with great determination. Finn worked not to be seen. He found himself cornered in the hat section.

"Hey," said a little boy, looking up at Finn with awe and wonder. "Are you him?"

"Go away!" Finn told the kid, not wanting to be bothered.

"But it's you, right?" the little boy asked. He stepped closer, sucked in a chest full of air, closed his eyes, and marched right into Finn. Finn stumbled back as the boy fell over.

"Wow!" the boy said, recovering and coming to his feet. "You're *real!*"

The little boy's attempt gave Finn an idea.

The Emporium sold clothing. Finn spotted a rack

of DHI merchandise, including the outfit that his own host character wore.

He snagged a pair of loud purple shorts and a green surfing shirt and pulled them over his own shirt and shorts. He didn't like leaving his Devil Rays cap behind, but saw little choice.

He placed his sunglasses into the empty pocket of his own shorts.

Two of the band members saw him and turned. Finn squeezed between them and ran.

Several kids spotted him at once. Shouting for autographs, they followed after him. Parents played catch-up, hollering after their kids, "Stop!" and "Get back here!"

Finn led the children out onto the sidewalk and into Main Street. An alarm sounded loudly as Finn left the store in clothing that hadn't been paid for. Anxious parents clogged the door, blocking the security guys.

"Hey!" one of the kids shouted above all the others. "Check it out! Two of them!"

Finn glanced over, only to realize he was standing twenty feet from his own DHI. His host self was surrounded by a pair of families and was answering questions.

The two band musicians stumbled out onto the

street. They looked back and forth from one Finn to the other. Which was which?

The real Finn pointed to the castle. He recited the memorized tour information recorded during the filming at Disney-MGM Studios. The DHI Finn, the hologram, not far away, mimicked the same moves and recited the same words from the same script.

Unable to determine which Finn to pursue, the band members froze. The real Finn then moved his small group of followers up the street at the exact same pace as his DHI. The two were perfect duplicates of each other.

Then, with enough distance between himself and his pursuers, Finn slipped down a side path. He quickly shed the DHI-Finn T-shirt and dumped it into the trash. He hopped out of the ugly shorts, slipped his sunglasses back on, and made off at a run, headed for the Haunted Mansion.

Ten minutes later, Finn spotted Amanda waiting on a bench near the Haunted Mansion's exit, as planned. A neat apron of lawn surrounded the towering brick Victorian-style structure. The paved area in front of the entrance was divided with chains and stanchions into three lanes, including one for the holders of the Fastpass. Parked against the mansion's front wall, equidistant between the entrance and exit, stood a gleaming all-black horse-drawn hearse—even the windows were black. The harness hung in midair; the horse was invisible.

Finn waited briefly before approaching Amanda, taking time to determine if either of them had been followed.

"Hey, there you are," Amanda said.

"I was spotted. I got away, but just barely."

"Will they bust you?"

"Not sure they can without catching me first, without proving it's me."

She glanced around. "So what now? How do we get you out of the park without your being caught?"

Finn hadn't thought through this possibility when forming their original plan. "I suppose they might watch the exit."

"You think? Get a life! Of course they will."

"There's a guy . . . an old guy. I think he might help, if I can find him." Finn spotted a pair of clean-cut young men approaching the Fastpass entrance, not thirty feet away, just on the other side of the hearse. He and Amanda moved a few feet to be screened from view.

Finn said, "Okay. Look over my shoulder. See those two tall guys in line? They've got wires in their ears, and I'll bet they're looking for me. And guess what? We're trapped."

Amanda studied the two. With Finn's back to them, at this distance, he was safe. She looked at the Haunted Mansion, then at the way the exit line converged toward the entrance line, the two separated by only a chain. "We can't leave through the exit line. Not with them there."

"I know."

"But they're pretty far back in the entrance line," she observed.

Finn's skin was crawled. How to explain any of this to his parents? "So we're trapped. I already had that much figured out."

"But they're just standing there, waiting."

"So?" Finn asked.

"So, we've got to get them to move," she answered.

"And how are we supposed to do that?" he asked sarcastically. "Call them on their radios and tell them they're wanted somewhere else?"

Amanda's brow knit tightly, deep in thought. "They'll move if they see you."

"What? Are you crazy?"

"Shush," she cautioned him. "Come on!" she said, taking him by the hand. He wasn't sure why, but he let her take charge. There was something about her confidence that reassured him. It felt almost as if she'd been through this kind of thing before—the way she stayed so calm; the way she studied the situation carefully. She led Finn quickly under a chain, behind the hearse, then between it and a low brick retaining wall. She peered around the hearse, monitoring the two security guards. "When I say, 'Go,' we go," she instructed.

"Ah—" Finn said, having second thoughts.

Amanda watched. The line was moving along, but the two security guys remained near the Mansion's entrance.

"Go!" she hissed.

Together they hurried into the open, ducked under a chain, and cut into the entrance line. A bunch of people moaned and groaned. A few openly complained. But as the line surged, Amanda and Finn moved with it.

Amanda was no giant, but she was an inch taller than Finn. She rose onto her tiptoes, looked back, and warned, "Okay . . . here they come." She tightened her hold on Finn's hand. Together, they moved with the line, which surged again. A few seconds later, they were inside the Mansion. Amanda kept watch behind them.

Finn and Amanda stepped into the Stretching Room—a hexagonal space twenty feet across. Portraits hung on the walls. Finn had just begun to feel safe, when, as Amanda tensed, he looked back and saw the two security guys enter—the last two people into the Stretching Room before its doors closed.

Amanda rose up. "Uh-oh," she said.

"What?"

"They're pushing their way over here."

The Stretching Room, jam-packed with people, did not make movement easy.

A loud voice boomed over the speakers, welcoming the visitors to the mansion. It warned them not to lean against the walls. The lights dimmed. Finn didn't need to stand on his tiptoes to see the two blond heads coming toward them.

Amanda pulled Finn down into a crouch. Together, they ducked and moved through the crowd. It seemed that the floor was beginning to sink. It looked and felt as if they were going down, down, down, in an elevator. The walls stretched. The ceiling receded above them. Even the oil paintings stretched longer.

"We're cooked," Finn said.

"No," Amanda said, still leading him. "We're okay." They reached a far wall.

Finn glanced back. The two guys were still pushing through the crowd toward them. "You're dreaming."

"We'll use the chicken door," she said.

"The what?"

"When I was something like five years old, I completely freaked out in here. Screamed my lungs out. Totally lost it."

As she said this, the room's floor stopped moving, the painted portraits now stretched grotesquely. A dead man dangled from a noose attached to the ceiling. Some kids shrieked.

Amanda continued, "My mom got me out without having to ride the Doom Buggies. It's called the chicken door."

"Here they come!" Finn cautioned in a whisper. But just as he said it, the crowd surged, pressing Finn against Amanda.

"Perfect timing," she said, smiling.

The two security guys got stuck in the jam, still a few yards away.

One of the wall panels opened like a door. The crowd—fat people, sweaty people, smelly people, bald people, and two teenage kids—lunged ahead.

The moment the door opened, Amanda took Finn by the hand and tugged. They hurried out into the dimly lit corridor leading to the Doom Buggies.

"Run!" Amanda whispered. "We have to hurry." She led him through an unmarked door immediately to the right. Finn found himself in a narrow, dimly lit corridor. Ghoulish sounds in the distance. Amanda ran, with Finn following closely behind her. She proved herself a very fast runner. It's almost as if she's flying, he thought.

Seconds later, they headed through yet another door. Outside again, they were only a few yards from where they'd been sitting only minutes earlier, the black hearse and the Fastpass line to their right. The entrance/exit was straight ahead.

The air came alive with the sound of piped-in music and the steady rumble of park guests talking.

Amanda glanced back at the Mansion. Her eyes went wide, and he knew they were in trouble. She practically pulled his arm off as she drew him into a small gift shop. They ducked behind a carousel of postcards.

The two security guys hurried past, only seconds behind them.

Finn stood beside Amanda, their arms touching.

"They've gone," she said. "We lost them."

Finn held up his father's camera. "Let's try to get a few more shots on our way out."

"But you gotta help us!" Finn pleaded.

"Listen, I can't," said Brad, the Imagineer who had produced the DHI film shoot at MGM-Disney. Behind him the soundstage hummed with forklifts moving equipment around.

From the Magic Kingdom, Amanda and Finn had ridden a bus to the Transportation and Ticket Center, and then another to Disney-MGM. It was late in the afternoon now, going on evening. Finn had to get home soon or face being grounded.

Brad looked at Amanda a couple times. "Do I know you?" he finally inquired.

"She's a friend," Finn said, interrupting before Amanda could answer.

Again Finn showed him one of the four images on the digital camera. "That's Willa. Remember? You must know how to find her. It's important."

"Your parents could make a formal request, I suppose."

"Yeah, right! My parents?" Finn complained. "It's not like I'm a stalker! I want a phone number, is all. Her school. Anything."

Brad shook his head, said he was sorry, and stepped back onto the soundstage. Finn called out loudly, "What if I can prove there's something wrong with the DHI technology?" This was his last resort.

Brad slowed a step, but did not stop completely.

"What if the DHIs are all in danger?"

Amanda and Brad looked at Finn curiously.

"What are you talking about, kid? There's nothing wrong with the technology," he said, taking a step closer.

"No?" Finn thought he had him now. "Get me the names of their schools. I'll do the rest."

"What's wrong with the technology? There's nothing wrong with the technology," Brad said more forcefully. "Nice try." He turned his back on Finn once again.

Finn said, "An old guy named Wayne. An Imagineer, like you."

"Wayne Kresky? How do you know Wayne?" Brad sounded impressed.

"That's for me to know and you to find out. Call Wayne. Ask him if he knows me."

"You know Wayne," Brad repeated, somewhat astonished.

"I know about the Overtakers."

The color in Brad's face drained away. Finn thought if he'd pushed him he would have fallen over.

"The sooner you clear this with Wayne, the better. The longer it takes for me to get to the other hosts, the greater the danger."

Brad's voice cracked as he said, "No one is in danger."

Finn said, "Talk to Wayne."

Finn signaled Amanda with his eyes: *time to go.*

A few minutes later they walked past the giant replica of Mickey's sorcerer's cap.

"What was that all about?" she asked. "What school do the Overtakers play for?"

"School?"

"They're a sports team, right?"

"Oh . . . Right." Finn said. He felt he owed her more than that. "Have you ever had a dream so real that when you woke up you were sure you'd just been wherever you'd been in the dream?"

"Everybody has dreams like that. For me . . . well . . . it's more like a nightmare."

"But what if somebody tells you something in the dream, something to look for when you wake up, and you wake up, and there it is?"

"I'd have to think about that," she conceded.

Finn felt frustrated. He wanted to be alone, with time to think things through.

She said, "If you know this guy Wayne, maybe he could help you find the others."

"No. He's the one that asked me to find them."

Amanda's face twisted. "Oh."

They reached the bus pickup point at the Transportation and Ticket Center. Her bus arrived.

She said, "The Overtakers aren't a sports team, are they?"

"No."

"And you're not going to tell me what they are."

"Maybe sometime."

"I can help you, Finn. I want to help you. But you've got to let me in."

He saw something behind her eyes, as if she knew more than she was letting on. Or was that just another girl trick? Finn couldn't think what to say.

Amanda climbed onto the bus, pausing briefly to talk to the driver. There were no tickets required on the Disney buses, so why would Amanda stop to talk to the driver? As the bus pulled away, Finn couldn't get the driver's face out of his mind: an old man with white hair, ice-blue eyes, and a kind face.

Wayne? Was it possible?

His hand trembling, Finn reread the list that had been left for him at the school office the next day:

Howard

Lee

Maitland

Jackson

He recognized these as the names of four middle schools. Four schools where he now believed he'd find the other DHIs. The note wasn't signed, but he knew it was from Brad.

"You don't have to do this," he reminded Amanda, though it was a little late now. They were riding a somewhat smelly city bus toward Lee Middle School. One-story buildings painted pink, sea blue, and white streamed past. Heat waves shimmered from the pavement. Another fall day.

"I'm okay," she replied.

He wanted to think this had been his idea, but he knew better. He wasn't sure how she'd managed to talk him into letting her join him, but here she was.

"We might not get back in time for fifth period," he warned. They'd skipped out on lunch together, slipping out a door near the gym. They'd be in some serious trouble if caught.

"I'm a big girl, Finn."

The bus driver, a fat guy with a blotchy red face, kept an eye on them in the mirror. Finn was feeling paranoid. "Hey, do you think—?"

"That he's watching us?" Amanda said, interrupting. "Yes."

"What if he's some kind of spy?" Finn asked.

"Oh, please. He's just curious about a couple of kids on their own in the middle of the day."

He felt stupid for having said that.

To drum it in, Amanda asked, "What kind of spy? For whom?" She whispered into his ear, "The Overtakers?"

She meant to tease him, but Finn wasn't laughing.

"You saw those guys yesterday at the Magic Kingdom," Finn reminded her.

"You weren't supposed to be there. You broke the rules," she reminded him. "You think they're Overtakers?" Again, she was teasing.

"As if you'd know."

"When are you going to tell me what's going on?"

"When I find out myself," he answered.

"These other kids. The other DHIs," she said. "You think they have the answers?"

"Not exactly."

The driver picked up a black radio microphone with a curly black cord and spoke into it. They couldn't hear what he was saying.

"What if he works with truancy cops?" Finn said. The schools were serious about kids cutting class.

"Now you're making me paranoid," she said sharply. She reached up and pressed the signal for the next stop. The brakes hissed as the bus slowed and pulled over to the curb.

As they hurried off the bus, Finn caught the driver's gaze in the side mirror: he was watching them.

Nine hot blocks later they reached the school. Finn was thirsty.

It was a nicer, newer school than theirs. They walked down the main hall, trying to look like they knew where they were going. Neither had been here before.

"What's the plan?" Amanda asked.

"We're here at lunchtime for a reason," Finn explained, checking a wall clock. They had to catch a return bus within twenty minutes or they'd miss the start of fifth period. He doubted they'd make it.

They located the cafeteria by following the noise and smells. To save time, Finn and Amanda had decided to split up. The enormous room was packed with kids and littered with backpacks. Hundreds of kids ate at long tables.

As Finn passed a table, he heard someone behind him say, "Hey, isn't that one of the hosts from Disney World?" Less than five minutes, and he'd been spotted. He didn't like being famous as much as he thought he would. He slipped on his sunglasses.

He saw Amanda a few tables away. She carried copies of the photographs they'd taken at the Magic Kingdom. She was showing them around to kids and asking questions. Finn didn't know which of the four DHIs went to Lee. He walked slowly, studying faces at the various tables.

It was really loud in here. An abundance of food smells combined into a stink he found sickening.

A big guy suddenly jumped up in Finn's way, an eighth-grader, judging by his size. He wore a Colorado Avalanche jersey, colorful jams, and new Nikes. "Who you staring at?" he growled.

"No one."

The big kid reached out and lifted Finn's sunglasses. "Think you're too cool?" Seeing Finn, he did a double take.

"Hey! How come I know you?"

"Give me back my glasses, please."

"Aren't you like on *Zoom* or something?"

"I'd like my glasses back, please."

"Give 'em back, Roy," a girl at the next table said. "It's not *Zoom*, stupid. He's a host—over at the Magic Kingdom—like Charlene Turner."

Charlene *Turner*. Finn had her last name now.

"Oh, yeah!" the big kid said, reluctantly returning the sunglasses to Finn. "What are you doing here?"

"Looking for Charlene," Finn said.

"Can't help you," the big guy said, sitting back down.

Finn looked to the girl expectantly, but she shook her head. "Sorry," she said.

Finn looked up to see Amanda waving at him. Having won his attention, she pointed to a window that looked out onto the playing fields. She moved her hand to mimic dribbling a basketball.

Leave it to Amanda: she'd found Charlene.

Charlene was talking with three other girls, all dressed for P.E. in gray gym shorts and yellow T-shirts. Charlene's expression changed instantly as she saw Finn approaching. He wondered why she should be so disappointed to see him. They'd gotten along well enough during the shoot.

"Hey," he said, greeting her, suddenly made painfully aware of Amanda standing by his side.

Charlene excused herself from her friends, saying, "Back in a whack," and approached Finn.

"What are you doing here? Are you cutting?" she asked, viewing Finn skeptically. "And who's she?"

"I have to talk to you," he said. Then, "She's a friend."

Charlene looked him over, and then met eyes with Amanda. "I don't think so," she said, and started to walk back toward her friends.

"The dreams. Disney after dark," Finn said. That stopped her cold.

Amanda looked at Finn curiously, but knew better than to say anything.

"Dreams that aren't dreams," he added.

Charlene spun to face him, excitement and alarm in her sparkling eyes. "No way you could know that," she said.

"Unless . . ." Finn said. "I've been there, too."

"What's this about?" Amanda asked. A whisper meant only for Finn, yet Charlene overheard.

"Where's she fit in?" Charlene asked.

"I told you: a friend willing to help me out," Finn explained. He added quickly, "Wayne, the old guy. Have you met him? He needs us all together. At night. Tonight, or tomorrow. As soon as I can find everyone: the five of us, all together."

"This isn't happening," said Charlene, suspicious of Amanda, puzzled by Finn. But the expression on her face told him she'd also been in the park in her dreams.

Charlene was the kind of girl you might see on a cereal box.

"Do you know how to reach any of the others?" Finn asked.

"I run into Willa on VMK sometimes, though it's more by chance." Virtual Magic Kingdom, a new "massively multiplayer" online game, was all the rage.

Finn played too. "Can you tell her to meet us?"

"It's not like I know her like that." Her friends called over to her. "Listen, I can't do this now," Charlene said.

"Contact Willa if you can. But whatever you do, go to bed early tonight. Eight o'clock. Eight o'clock, exactly."

"I've been trying to stay up. I don't exactly love my dreams lately."

"We need to know," he said. She had to be as curious about this as he was. Could they possibly meet in the park in their dreams?

"Yeah, okay . . ." Charlene said reluctantly.

Charlene looked straight at Amanda but spoke to Finn. "*No one* can know about this," she said. Then she lowered her voice and hissed, "It isn't safe."

The coach's whistle sounded shrilly. Charlene took off running but glanced back at Finn one last time. He saw fear in her eyes.

"Meet me!" he called out.

Charlene didn't answer, but her eyes registered that she'd heard.

After a moment, Amanda said, "We'd better be getting back."

"Yeah," Finn agreed.

"*It isn't safe.*"

Charlene's warning seemed to hang in the air between them.

"I'm going to bed," Finn announced, standing up from the dinner table and carrying his plate to the kitchen sink. He hadn't been to bed at this hour since elementary school.

"Are you not feeling well?" His mother said, in shock.

"I'm feeling fine," he said. "I'm just going to bed early, if that's all right?"

"Have you finished your homework?"

"Yes, it's done. I stayed after for study hall."

"You what?" She set down a bowl of mashed potatoes and crossed her arms. "Finn?" She eyed him suspiciously. "You stayed after school to do your homework, and now you're heading to bed at seven-fifteen?" The night before last, his mother had received a call from her contact on the DHI team, asking if Finn had been to the Magic Kingdom lately. Finn had denied going, feeling awful about lying, but knowing she wouldn't believe him. She'd grounded him. Finn didn't even try to challenge her, and that had convinced her of his guilt. "If you're planning to sneak out—"

"No way!" Finn said. "I'm not, I promise." He

stepped forward and kissed her. "Good night, Mom."

"I'm going to check on you when your father gets home."

"Okay," Finn said. "Just don't wake me up. Please," he added. "I need a good night's sleep."

He checked his computer. No interesting e-mail. He debated logging on to VMK and looking for Charlene, but instead he changed into his pajamas and brushed his teeth, passing his mother in the hall on the way back from the bathroom.

She wore her concern openly. "It's only seven-fifteen," she reminded him. "We could catch the Simpsons."

She'd trapped him. This was an offer he would never normally turn down.

"I'm going to pass, Mom, but thanks."

"It's a bad rule, making you get approval before going. A stupid rule, really. If you . . . if you took a friend to the park . . . well . . . your father and I would understand how you wouldn't have wanted to tell us."

Finn considered her olive branch. "Amanda," he said. "Her name's Amanda."

Relief spread across his mother's face. He feared she might hug him.

She was smiling now. Beaming.

"'Night, Mom."

She looked like she might cry.

"I'll talk to your father," was all she said.

Finn knew he wouldn't be grounded by morning.

He shut his bedroom door. If he crossed over into the park, he didn't want to be in his pajamas, so he changed back into jeans and a T-shirt. He lay there for fifteen wakeful minutes with the lights out, checking the clock regularly. He tried to relax. Dusk played at the edges of his shades. It felt like the middle of the day. He cleared his mind, dozed off, and finally sank into a deep sleep.

"You're learning," said the old man's voice from behind him.

Finn turned to see Wayne, in khakis and a plaid shirt, sitting behind the wheel of an electric golf cart with the Walt Disney World logo painted on the front. The sky glowed faintly on the horizon. It took Finn a moment to register his location as somewhere in Frontierland, not far from Tom Sawyer Island.

"You just missed the fireworks display," Wayne said, stopping the cart alongside Finn. "Park closed a few minutes ago. I love this time of night. Especially the music."

"What music?" Finn didn't hear any music and

realized now that he'd always heard music in the park. The old guy was a bit daffy.

Finn reached out and grabbed the steel bar that supported the cart's awning. He saw his glowing hand wrap around the metal but could also faintly see *through* his hand as well. Not only that, but the metal didn't feel exactly like metal.

"This is so weird," he confessed.

"Don't fight it," Wayne said.

"This is probably the weirdest thing I've ever done. And I've done some weird stuff," Finn said. "This one time, a friend of mine and I—" He caught himself blabbering. Instead, he told Wayne, "I found Charlene. I'm still trying to locate the others."

"It has to be all of you. You understand that, don't you? All or nothing. Youngsters your age, you always think it's all about you, only you. I can promise you, it has to be all of you."

"I want to help you."

"You have no choice," he said. "At some point you'll understand that."

Finn felt the words like drumbeats in his chest. "What do you mean?"

"You know what I mean."

"I thought it was a dream at first," Finn said.

"And now?"

"Now I don't think so. I don't know exactly what it is if it isn't a dream, but I don't think it could be a dream." He hesitated and said, "I saw the moon."

Wayne nodded and cocked his head curiously. "Yet something's bothering you."

"Charlene said it isn't safe. You basically said the same thing."

"And yet here you are. You came back," Wayne said.

"You brought me back."

"Did I? Not exactly. This is a two-way street, young man. You're neither hologram nor human. You're something in between, I think. The holograms don't think for themselves, and they speak only what you recorded for them. How much you are . . . one or the other . . . may depend on your thinking—what you're thinking, how you're thinking it. So I'd be careful of what I was thinking, if I were you."

Finn spotted a large gold bear by the entrance to the Jungle Cruise. He shook his head to clear his eyes since the bear was walking on two feet and there was what looked like an oversized rat jogging to keep up with it. "Is that . . . ?"

"What?" the old man said excitedly.

"Pooh and Piglet?"

"Is it?"

"There!" Finn said, pointing.

"I told you, didn't I?" Wayne was quick to lose his patience. "I don't see what you see." He sounded frustrated.

"Pooh and Piglet." Finn was certain now.

"What are they doing?"

"Walking away from us."

"Anything else?"

"You're kidding, right?" Finn felt like some kind of translator.

"I told you: things are happening in the park. We—you and your friends, actually—need to stop them."

"The Overtakers."

"Yes."

"It isn't safe," Finn repeated.

"No, it's not," Wayne said, agreeing.

"What's that mean, exactly?"

"What did you think of the park as a small child?"

"Magic," Finn said without a second thought. He still thought of it as magic.

"Exactly," Wayne agreed. "But there are two sides to magic, yes? Good magic is what you're talking about. But there's other magic besides good magic."

"Black magic," Finn stated.

"A layman's term, but yes, a darker side to magic that few if any fully understand."

"Do you?"

"Heavens no. But Walt did. He wrote about it. He made films. Invented characters. He understood its seriousness, its potential for . . . but we're getting ahead of ourselves."

"Potential for what? Evil?"

"Let's just put a pin in that. We'll come back to it."

Finn climbed into the front seat of the golf cart. His feet disappeared. They weren't simply in shadow; they were . . . gone. He felt a little faint. "My feet," he gasped.

Wayne explained, "The hologram imaging system isn't set up to project to all locations. There are places we call shadows. Like dead spots where cell phones don't work. Inside some attractions they will be visible—*you*, the DHIs, will be visible. Other locations, maybe not. Your feet inside a cart, for instance," he said, pointing, "not so good. You may be able to control this. We don't know for sure. You're the first of your kind."

Finn glanced down at his missing feet. It wasn't so bad.

"Okay?" Wayne asked.

"Okay, I guess."

Wayne pressed the accelerator. The cart lurched forward.

"Where'd you get your license?" Finn asked, holding on for dear life.

"What license?" Wayne answered, his eyes sparkling.

Four or five dark, shadowy figures streaked across the intersection in front of the cart. Wayne didn't see them. Finn reached over and jerked the cart's steering wheel, narrowly averting an accident. Wayne braked to a stop.

"You nearly paved those guys," Finn exclaimed.

"What guys?"

"The—" Finn couldn't complete the sentence. Wayne hadn't seen them. Then Finn said, "Pirates." He pointed to their left. "But not exactly pirates. They look more like . . ."

"Like what?"

"More like robots . . . Like the lifelike pirates in Pirates of the Caribbean. And Finn realized that was it: they weren't people, but Audio-Animatronics figures that had somehow come alive. "Never mind," Finn said, not wanting to sound crazy. A group of the figures was pushing a line of small blue cars ahead of them. Finn thought he recognized the cars but couldn't associate them with any particular attraction. He was stuck on the idea that some of the AAs—but they were only *machines*—had come *alive. Was that possible?*

Wayne asked, "How many?"

"Five . . . no, six, including the guy with the hat."

"Interesting. What guy with a hat?"

Finn didn't want to go there. He'd call them pirates and that was that. "You really can't see them?"

"Me? Heavens, no. I see the cars, but nothing else," Wayne said excitedly. "And if you can see them, then maybe you can stop them. Or at least *try* to stop them."

"Stop them from what, exactly?"

"Three nights ago at the end of the Fantasmics show, the dragon set Mickey on fire. Obviously, that's not supposed to happen. Mickey is supposed to win. He jumped into the water. He's all right. The crowd laughed. They didn't get it. But Mickey could have . . . He could have . . . could be in some serious trouble. And then what?"

"But those are actors, right?"

"The dragon is a machine, an Audio-Animatronics machine. But that machine malfunctioned, didn't it? It did something that it's not programmed to do. How is that possible? How can that be explained?"

Finn thought, What a strange old man.

Wayne said, "You think I'm a strange old man."

"Do not."

"You're the chosen leader of the DHIs. Don't question it. Accept it. Without you, Finn, there is no plan."

"What plan?" Finn gulped. Wayne seemed so serious all of a sudden.

Finn sensed something behind and to his right. He spun around and saw her. Charlene.

His breath caught. She was . . . glowing. A fuzzy light sputtered at the edges of her body and all around her head, like a halo. She wore a white nightgown. Her hair danced in the wind.

Some distance behind her stood Philby. He wore school clothes, like Finn. Finn recognized him immediately. They were missing Maybeck and Willa.

"Hey there!" a gruff voice called out.

Finn turned. The pirate in the black hat was addressing him.

Me? Finn's expression said, though he kept his mouth shut.

Wayne asked, "What's happening? Don't get ahead of yourself," he warned.

Charlene and Philby moved steadily closer.

Wayne, appearing distraught, admonished Finn. "You must not get ahead of yourself!"

Finn climbed out of the golf cart. Then, concentrating, he walked right *through* the cart to the other side. It's all about what I'm thinking, he realized. If I focus on being a DHI, I'm nothing but light.

A shimmering Charlene approached a tree. She tried to walk through, but crashed into it instead. "How'd you do that?" she asked. "Why can't I do it?" she asked Wayne.

Wayne seemed flustered. "You all need more time." He glared at Finn.

The harsh grinding of metal dragging on pavement interrupted them as the pirates pushed the line of blue cars.

The one in the hat, with a broad moustache and thick black beard, hollered out, "Ahoy, there, matie! Lend us a hand, if you will."

Finn stayed where he was.

"I said lend a hand!" hollered the elaborately dressed man. Behind him, the more scruffy pirates—*machines!*—pushed and dragged the blue cars. All of a sudden, Finn recognized them as the cars from the Buzz Lightyear ride. He'd been on it dozens of times.

"I'll pass, thank you," Finn said.

"Pass? I gave ye an order, me boy. Now heave to!" the captain growled.

"An order? I don't think so." Finn replied.

Charlene stepped back and dragged Philby with her. They ducked behind the tree.

"The name's Blackbeard," the man said. His mouth moved like a puppet's. His arms and legs moved stiffly. His eyes mechanically shifted, from the left to the right, their motion disconnected from his speech.

Finn felt a spike of fear but hid it. "Is that so? And I suppose I'm Jack Sparrow?" he asked, smirking.

61

The captain stepped forward boldly, still a ways off. "Is ye now?"

The pirates stopped their pushing. They gathered behind their captain.

Finn counted six in all. They were dressed in ill-fitting costumes. They had scars on their faces and scabs on their hairy legs. They went barefoot, wearing dark pants that stopped at their calves, and blue-and-white striped shirts. But they weren't human.

Blackbeard drew his sword. His six pirates drew knives. "I said lend a hand. You're my conscript now, lad. I'd be obliged if you hove to."

"You're not ready," Wayne hissed at Finn from the shadows. "I'd help you if I could see them, but I can't."

Finn felt a jolt of terror, unsure what to do. His legs, wobbly and rigid, were unwilling to move. He figured he could run faster than a bunch of mechanical pirates but wasn't sure he wanted to test that theory. Besides, he couldn't budge.

Finn looked back. Four glowing eyes, like cats' eyes, shone from behind a tree. Charlene and Philby.

"What are you doing with those cars?" Finn asked the captain, stalling. *Think!*

"You might could say I'm borrowing them, laddie. Or you might could say the Space Ranger Spin is under repair." He tilted his head and cast an evil eye in Finn's direction. "I've seen you before, Jack Sparrow. Now, where would that be?"

"I don't believe we've met," Finn said.

"He's one a' them hosts, Captain," a smallish man with frog eyes called out. The man's right arm continually lifted up and down, up and down. This was apparently the motion he made in his role in the attraction, and he couldn't stop it.

"A host!" the captain declared. "A new ride? Is that what ye're telling me?"

His pirates mumbled.

"We don't much care for new rides," the captain explained in a dry, cold voice. "Don't much care for them at all."

"Do I look like a ride?" Finn asked. His voice trembled. "I'm just a boy."

"You're *my* boy now," the captain declared. "Ain't he, lads?" His pirates all nodded in chorus. He said to Finn, "Now . . . be a good boy and lend us a hand."

"I'd prefer not to," Finn said. "If you don't mind, I'll be on my way." He summoned his courage and turned.

"Ye don't turn yer back on the captain, youngster! I said *halt!*"

Finn stopped and glanced back over his shoulder. The captain signaled his crew, and they reacted immediately, like a bunch of well-trained dogs. They fanned out.

They were not exactly fast on their mechanical legs and feet, but they were steady and worked well as a team.

One of the pirates climbed into a Space Ranger car. He aimed its toy laser cannon at Finn and fired. A bright red pulse of light shot through the night, narrowly missing Finn. He'd ridden the Space Ranger Spin himself a dozen times or more. He knew there was nothing to fear; he'd put his hands into the laser's light stream before. Nothing ever happened. The laser cannons were no more dangerous than a flashlight.

Another thin red line of light flashed. Again, it missed.

But then Finn realized the cars were not plugged in, were not attached to any ride, had no power source. So where did the electricity for the cannon come from?

As if to answer him, the next pinpoint of light struck his arm. A red bead flickered on his shirtsleeve. The fabric instantly turned brown, then gray. Then . . . *ouch!*

It burned him! Finn leaped out of the way.

"Hey!" he blurted out.

He smelled burning hair. His hair. His skin.

The laser was *real.*

Another flash. Finn dodged out of the way. He avoided the next few attempts as well, the red beams flying past him like glowing arrows. He danced left and right, his arm stinging.

Now the other pirates circled and closed in on Finn, their knives extended.

If a toy laser can burn, what is a very real-looking knife going to do? Wayne had warned him that he was half hologram, half human. Only now did he realize his human half could hurt.

His wounded arm looked less transparent all of a sudden. He wondered if his fear made him more human than hologram. He pushed against the fear, as if he were trying to shut a heavy door.

A gray-haired pirate with a peg leg *thump*, *thump*, *thumped* his way closer. The circle closed around him. Now Finn could smell the pirates: oily, like an old car, and faintly electrical.

Charlene called out to him from behind the tree.

The captain raised his sword higher, trying to follow that voice. "Reinforcements, mates! Be ye ready!"

Two of the younger pirates closed in on Finn. They walked stiffly and slowly, like six-foot-tall toy soldiers. Finn circled to his right, away from them. He dodged two more attempts from the laser. One of the pirates was hit in the process; the captain raised his hand to stop the laser assault.

The two young pirates, their knives glinting, pressed ever closer.

The captain, with one knee cocked, his foot perched

on the lead car, thundered, "Well, now, laddies! Serve him up like a fine filet!"

"Hey, dog breath!" It was Philby. He stepped out from behind the tree.

All six pirates turned toward Philby at once.

With the pirates' attention briefly diverted, Finn sprang for the nearest Space Ranger car. He grabbed hold of its laser, swiveled and fired. A pulse of red light shot out. Finn was a veteran of Space Ranger Spin. He winged the pirate in the car ahead of him, not ten feet away. The pirate didn't seem to feel it—he *was* a machine.

Another pirate charged. Finn shot his knee out, and the thing toppled over, its one good leg moving, still trying to walk.

Finn saw a difference between Blackbeard and the other pirates: Blackbeard had a vaguely human sound to him. Most of the others—all but a few—looked and sounded more like machines than real pirates.

Finn sliced and burned right through the peg leg of the older pirate. He too, teetered, leaned, and tumbled over. Two down.

On the captain's command, his men charged as a unit. Finn aimed for their knees in a brilliant display of gunnery. They staggered. Several fell. The captain ordered a retreat, and Finn held his fire.

Blackbeard, his eyes darting weirdly back and forth, reached for, but then decided against, the sword that hung at his waist. He clucked his tongue in disappointment. "Ye've made a terrible mistake, lad. Me advice for ye is, go back from whence you came. And take them there other two with ye. For yer own good." His mechanical facial expression never changed. He made no more threats—not with Finn still perched behind the laser. He simply turned and walked away. He did not run, did not hurry, Finn noted. He headed down the path and, a moment later, was gone, out of sight. His pirates dragged themselves and their other fallen mates off with them.

Finn released his hold on the laser, his fingers stiff from gripping so tightly. His shirt bore a small charred hole. The burn on his arm was now a blistered scab. He'd hoped he might only have imagined it—but no: it hurt something fierce.

He climbed out of the car.

"Way to go," Charlene said simply, trying not to sound too impressed.

Philby approached, and Finn thanked him for the diversion.

The two shook hands. It felt to Finn as if that handshake represented a pact between them. They were in this together now.

To celebrate what he called their "first victory," Wayne offered them ice-cream bars from a food kiosk. He carried a heavy-looking ring with dozens of keys of all shapes and sizes with which he unlocked the kiosk.

Finn sat down on a bench. Wayne handed him his ice-cream sandwich, and Finn tore off the paper and bit into the treat. He *tasted* it, though it wasn't nearly as sweet as it should have been. Maybe he was only half human, he thought.

"What about Willa and Maybeck?" Charlene asked, enjoying her ice cream.

Finn devoured the ice-cream sandwich. With his mouth full he said, "No clue."

Charlene explained, "Me and Philby met here in the park the other night. We haven't found each other . . . you know . . . on the outside yet. Not like the way you found me. But here we are."

Her mention of "the outside" sent shivers up Finn's spine.

Philby said, "I don't seem to remember as much as Charlene when I wake up. I'm not sure why. But you know, I've never really remembered my dreams, so maybe that's part of it."

"But this isn't a dream," Finn reminded him.

"I know that now," Philby said. "But I didn't know that earlier."

"This will all change," Wayne said. "The more you cross over, the more it will feel familiar to you."

"Cross over," Philby repeated.

"Weird, huh?" Finn said.

Wayne's hand slipped into his pocket.

"No!" Finn called out, knowing the man intended to send him back to his bed. "You owe us an explanation first."

"I need you all together," Wayne said.

Finn said, "You have the three of us. That will have to do. When—if—we're ever all together, then fine, you can explain it again. But I just got burned on my arm by a group of . . ."

"Pirates," Philby said. "Mechanical pirates."

"Mechanical pirates that could talk and take orders," Charlene added.

"Yes. *Pirates*," Finn said. "Pirates *you* can't see, as I understand it. And I *don't* understand it. And I'll stay up, dusk to dawn, if I have to, in order to figure this out. And, if you don't tell us what this is about, you won't see me again."

"Or me," Philby said.

"Or me," Charlene agreed.

"It's now or never," Finn declared.

The old man looked paler by a good deal. Some bird off in the thick of green cooed deeply. Finn felt like they were being watched.

"All right," Wayne said, smiling. He glanced around suspiciously. "Come with me."

They followed. After a bit of a walk, Wayne unlocked and admitted them into the auditorium for the Country Bear Jamboree. He placed the three kids in the first row. Then he walked through the dark space and checked all the doors. He returned to the front of the hall and leaned against the stage to address them.

"There's a fine line between imagination and reality. An inventor dreams something up, and pretty soon, it's there on the table before him. A science-fiction writer envisions another world, and then some space probe finds it. If you believe in something strongly enough, I think you can make it happen."

"That's a good thing," Finn said.

Wayne asked, "But what if we believe in witches and villains? If we believe as strongly in things like them . . . can we make them happen?"

"You're giving me the creeps."

"This park, this wonderful place, makes both sides happen—the good *and* the bad. Some of Walt's stories go back generations. Hundreds of years. *Cinderella. Snow White.* We see similar stories in many different cultures across the globe. What if these stories were once true? If they were real, passed down from generation to generation? Different cultures experiencing similar things? And if they were real, *are* real? If the hero and heroine go off to live happily ever after, then what happens to the villains, witches, sea monsters, and evil stepmothers?"

Finn said, "You're saying that because the park makes them real, they *are* real?"

"I'm saying if you believe strongly enough, anything can happen, and *millions* of people, kids and adults, visit this park—all the Disney parks, the cruise line, the Broadway shows, the Web sites, Disney on Ice—every year. And they—"

"Believe," Finn said.

"In the bad and the good," Charlene said.

"Exactly. Yes, they do. And there's power in that belief," Wayne said.

"So?" Philby asked.

"So you know your history. What is inevitable once evil gains power?"

Philby answered, "It wants more. Empires. Wars. That kind of stuff."

"We call them the Overtakers," Wayne whispered.

Finn felt the hairs on the back of his neck stand up.

"Who?" Philby asked, also in a whisper.

"We—the Imagineers, I'm talking about—needed something mortal, something part . . . a hybrid . . . that could cross over to the character world. That's what we call it: crossing over. We've suspected for years that the characters 'come alive'—if you will—once the gates are closed. We've had evidence of this for some time. But when the trouble started happening, we knew we needed . . . you—someone who could see the Overtakers. Interact with them. Stop them."

"This is crazy," Charlene mumbled.

"Walt knew the time would come. The world gets out of balance. The dark forces rule. History is full of such times. They can last hundreds of years unchecked. It's like a plague, this dark thought. There's no music. No art. Only tyranny and war. Madness."

Charlene said, "I think I've heard enough. I'd like to wake up now. *In my own bed.*"

Wayne continued, "You asked to hear this. So listen."

The kids remained seated, their full attention on Wayne.

"As I said, Walt knew such a time would come. He left us a treasure map, for a scavenger hunt, something the Overtakers could not easily figure out, even if they obtained it, which they never have. Most of them are machines, you see—audio-animatronics and figures from attractions. Only a handful can think, can communicate. But they control the others."

"The Stonecutter's Quill," Finn mumbled. Wayne had mentioned it the first time they'd met.

"The *what?*" Philby asked.

"It's a fable," Wayne said. "But I'm getting ahead of myself. We must wait for the others."

"I, for one," Charlene said, "am never coming back. So if you've got something to say, you'd better say it."

Wayne paced as he talked. "Think about it. The Pirates, Maleficent, Cruella DeVil, Ursula—all with so much belief fueling them, belief, to draw upon. It was inevitable, I suppose."

"*What* was inevitable?" Charlene asked.

Wayne didn't seem to hear her. "And so many others, all in the same place at the same time—here, in this park. The belief supporting them, making them stronger. Making them real."

Finn explained to Charlene and Philby, "This has something to do with the fire-breathing dragon and Mickey in Fantasmic."

Wayne said, "That's not the end of it. We have rides close unexpectedly. The laser cars go missing. Costumes disappear. The parade route is changed, with no one the wiser. Small, harmless stuff so far, but for how long? Did you see the news? A hundred padlocks were stolen from a hardware store. The security tapes revealed nothing, showed no one inside the store. Mark my word: those padlocks were stolen—one minute on the shelf, the next, missing. So, how'd that happen? How long until *the rest of us* can see them? How long until they can burn us the way they burned Finn tonight? What happens then? What happens when they realize there's a whole *big world* outside these park walls? What if they want to expand their empire? What then?" He stopped. He was red-faced and breathing hard. Finn thought he looked a little sick.

"Maybe you should sit down," Finn suggested.

"It wasn't until the hurricane that we realized how far this had come."

"The hurricane," Finn repeated softly.

"A hurricane changed course while out at sea and then headed directly here to Orlando. I'll accept that as coincidence, a fluke of nature." Wayne, clearly growing agitated, collected himself. "But do you know what happened to that storm *after* it passed over here? Check it out on the Internet. It *lost power*. Came in here at one strength and left considerably weaker. You think it just rained and blew itself out? We think not. We think that storm was harnessed. Used like a giant battery. Like a vampire sucking blood, the Overtakers used that storm to gain power. Since that storm, we've had a lot more unexplained inconveniences. They're practicing. They're getting ready for something bigger."

"Are you listening to yourself? That can't be," Finn mumbled. "That's crazy!"

Philby caught Finn's look. He shook his head as if to say: *It's not crazy.* Then he said aloud, "Some ancient civilizations are thought to have used powerful storms to control their people."

Wayne said, "That hurricane was downgraded after passing over here." He sounded frightened.

"I'd really like to go home now," Charlene said.

Finn thought about it for a moment and said softly, "So, let's say we accept some of this. What are we supposed to do?" He knew he sounded terrified, but he couldn't help himself.

"You three, *and* the others, were carefully chosen for your individual talents. As DHIs you are part of their world; as kids, you're part of ours. You are our eyes into the other side."

"Spies," Philby said.

"If you like," Wayne said.

"I don't like," Philby answered.

Finn sputtered, "I don't see what we're supposed to do."

"Sure you do, or you wouldn't be afraid. And while you're at it, think about this," Wayne said. "Why and how do you think we came up with the concept of the DHIs?"

Charlene said, "Us being hosts . . . You're saying that wasn't the real reason?"

Philby said, "They needed something that could exist in the character world but wasn't a part of it."

Wayne grinned at him. "Ah-ha!" he declared. "But the development costs. The time and energy it took to create you. We had to have a use for you to justify you to the rest of the company." He met eyes with Finn.

"Because no one would believe you if you told them a bunch of witches were going to take over the Magic Kingdom," Finn said.

Wayne didn't answer this directly. He said, "And so we dreamed up the idea of the holograms, the interactive hosts."

Philby suggested, "You needed spies, someone to find out what the Overtakers were up to."

"Find out if they even *existed*," Wayne said, nodding.

"And now that you know they do," Finn stated, rubbing the burn on his left arm, "now what?"

"We need to lure out their leader, whoever that turns out to be. *What*ever that turns out to be. Deprogram it? Redraw it? Lock it up? Who knows?"

"You need us as bait?" Finn complained.

"Walt left us a solution," Wayne reminded. "We

need you to solve the riddle of the Stonecutter's Quill." The old guy looked exhausted.

Charlene said, "And if we don't want to?"

Wayne's mouth twisted, and his eyes looked stern and serious. "At some point you're going to have to sleep," he said. "And from now on, when you do, you're going to cross over." He hesitated, then stepped closer to her, his face gentle and kind. "I'm sorry, my dear girl, but there is no skipping this ride."

When Finn awoke, he hurried into the bathroom, tore his shirt off over his head, and studied the pea-size red-and-brown scab with the dime-size scarlet circle of flesh that surrounded it. The burn hurt something fierce. This was no dream. He winced as he cleaned it with soap and water. "Yaaa!" he hollered, his cry echoing in the tiled room.

"Finn, dear?" his mother called from the hallway. She knocked. "Are you all right?"

"Fine!"

"May I come in?"

"Ah . . ."

She let herself in. She was in her nightgown. Dawn had arrived an hour earlier, the pink of the eastern sky now silver with clouds.

"Finn, dear?"

She studied him in the mirror's reflection, from behind, no doubt wondering why he was only half dressed, his shirt in a ball on the floor.

"What's *that*? What *happened*? Honey?" She laid her warm hand on his shoulder.

Finn felt like telling her the truth, but he knew she wouldn't believe him. So what to do?

They both were focused on the burn. He couldn't very well say that he'd been in a laser battle with invisible pirates. She'd cart him off to the mental ward, or worse, their minister.

"A cigarette," Finn said. He hated smoking more than anything on the planet. In her right mind, his mother knew this about him. Finn had once walked across a restaurant and boldly asked a smoker to put out his cigarette so that his own hamburger didn't have to taste like an ashtray. This, at seven years old. But his mother wasn't thinking right. To her, seeing was believing.

"You? What?" she gasped.

He felt awful, both for lying to her and for using smoking as his excuse. He'd crushed her. "Mom . . ."

"Who? How'd you get it?"

"Mom . . ."

"And don't you lie to me!"

He tried to think of how to explain this without lying, because not to lie was one promise he had made to his parents that he hated having to break. "I didn't smoke it, Mom! A cigarette . . . burned me." He bent and picked up his shirt off the floor and held it up to show to her. The hole was obvious enough. "It was this guy—a bully, you know."

She collected herself. "A bully? Who did this to you, Finn?"

"A pirate," he heard himself mumble.

"What?"

"He's . . . called 'Pirate' because he's so mean."

"He should be arrested."

"No! It's nothing."

"*Nothing?* That's a—criminal act—burning someone. Finn." She spun him around to face her. "Breathe."

"What?"

"I want to smell your breath."

"Mom!"

"Now, young man!"

He breathed toward her groping nose.

She blinked rapidly. "So after all we talked about, you sneaked out anyway?"

He'd forgotten about that part of his explanation. "I . . . ah . . ."

"Well!" she brightened. Her eyes went soft and her eyebrows danced, and he thought that this was the way she looked before she cried. "Oh, Finn. Thank you for not lying to me. It's *so* important not to lie." She added matter-of-factly, "Give me his name, please. His real name. Right now."

"I don't know his real name. Just some kid. I don't think he meant to burn me, just scare me a little. It's just one of those growing-up things, you know?" She often talked to him about "growing-up things."

She held him at arm's length now, studying him thoughtfully. He didn't like the look on her face. This was her best imitation of a lie detector.

"Did you *sleep* in your clothes?" The dark cloud in her eyes concerned him. "This is the same shirt—these are the same clothes you wore yesterday, for goodness' sakes!"

As she pieced it together, Finn tried to think of something to distract her. But she was too quick for him. "I don't remember that hole in your shirt at dinner."

"Hands beneath the table, Mom."

"Finn . . ."

"I can't help it if you didn't see it."

"I should have known, with your going to bed so early last night." She was thinking aloud. "We can't tell your father."

He breathed a huge sigh of relief.

She eyed his wound, "But this did happen to you *last night*, didn't it? *After* you went to sleep."

He had no choice but to nod. Being grounded for life was better than continuing to lie to her.

"How late were you out?" she asked, heading for his bedroom window to inspect it like a detective.

"Midnight." This was the truth.

"How'd you do it? Your father and I were down-stairs until eleven or later."

Finn's window looked down on an area of the drive-way in front of the garage. There was no roof below him, just a tiny apron of flower bedding and then the drive-way's black asphalt. He had a brain freeze trying to think up a way to explain his nocturnal escape, knowing from previous experience that the more of the story he made up, the more difficult it would be to keep it straight.

Then he remembered the room's window box. "The fire ladder!" he said. His grandfather had installed a chain fire ladder several years before. In the event of an emergency he was to block the bottom crack of his door with clothes or bedding and wait for instructions from firemen to use the stow-away ladder. He'd promised a long time ago to never use the ladder to sneak out.

"I see," she said, clearly disappointed in him.

"If you have to ground me, I understand," Finn said, trying to subtly encourage her to do so. If grounded, he could spend more time in his room without raising sus-picions. More time in his room meant more chances to sleep, and sleep meant crossing over. If he napped, would he cross over into the park during the day?

So many questions to answer.

"Show me!" his mother ordered.

"Show you what?"

"The ladder. How you got down there."

Finn looked out the window and felt a little dizzy. It looked about a hundred feet down. His mother knew he was afraid of heights.

"You want me to go down the ladder?" He knew she couldn't possibly want him to do that. It looked like a death wish.

Glancing out the window, she said, "No. It looks dangerous to me."

"It is dangerous."

She put her hand down onto the window box's lid.

He was in big trouble if she opened up the window box. That fire ladder was buried under a pile of unused toys that went back years. Probably dust an inch thick. How would he explain any of that?

He hurried to stop her. "I messed up, Mom! I'm sorry."

"You're definitely grounded."

"Yes, ma'am."

"And you're not to use that ladder except in case of an *emergency*. I need your word on that." She added hotly, "And I'll expect you to keep it."

"I promise." He hung his head, feeling a mixture of shame and excitement. He poked at his wound as if it hurt a lot more than it did.

"Now let's get that cleaned up!" she said.

10

Finn stood in front of his locker, wondering how he was going to find the remaining two DHIs, Willa and Maybeck. He didn't trust Charlene to seek out Willa. Just as he was thinking this, a voice said: "Isabella Angelo. They call her Willa." Amanda stepped out from behind his open locker door.

Where had she come from? Could she read minds?

"What? How?" Surprised by her, he couldn't get a sentence out.

"Willa," Amanda repeated.

Finn remembered Willa as a bookish girl with chocolate-brown eyes and a loud voice.

"You found her?" he asked, astonished.

"Maitland Middle School."

"But how—?"

"I have my ways," she said.

"She's into some weird kind of sport," Finn said, remembering. "It's not gymnastics."

"Archery."

"That's it!"

"Like cupid," she said. "And swimming." Amanda

had certainly done her homework. "She said you were cute."

"You've spoken to her?"

"She'll meet you in VMK tonight, like you suggested."

"You're amazing."

"How was it last night when you went to sleep?" she asked curiously. "Did you . . . you know?"

"What?" asked Dillard Cole from behind them. Dillard's sweatshirt was big enough to cover a chair.

"Hey, Dill. I'm kinda busy here."

Dillard looked between the two. His gaze landed on Finn. He looked hurt. He shuffled off. The sides of his shoes were so worn on the outside edges that his ankles rolled.

Finn felt bad to see Dillard so crushed. He was a good guy. The crossing over was taking Finn away from friends like Dill, making all sorts of trouble for him.

Amanda persisted. "Did you end up in the park last night or not?"

"Yeah. Charlene was there. And Philby. And there were . . . pirates."

"Pirates?"

"As in Pirates of the Caribbean. The machines—the guys you see in the ship, and stuff. It's kinda hard to explain, exactly."

The shock registered on her face, but dissipated just as quickly. "And?"

"It got a little . . . weird."

"Define *weird*," she said. "Did you see anyone else?"

"Like who?"

"I don't know."

Finn rolled his sleeve up past his elbow to the Band-Aid and the glowing red circle surrounding it. "I took a laser hit," he said.

Her face twisted. "That looks like a cigarette burn."

"You and my mother," he muttered.

"Excuse me?"

"I'm grounded. As in, forever. It's a long story."

She said, "Maybeck works at Crazy Glaze."

Finn looked at her blankly.

"The ceramics shop," she said. "Over on Kilgore. You decorate mugs and plates and pitchers. Stuff like that. They fire them there, too. It's his aunt's store."

"How do you know all this?" he asked.

She avoided an answer, blushing and staring at her feet. "I'm coming with you," she announced. "That's part of the deal."

"What deal?"

"Our deal."

"Do we have a deal?" he asked.

"We do now."

"Maybe you missed the part where I told you I was grounded. I gotta get home after school."

"Did you ride the bus?"

"My bike."

"Well, there you go," she said. "Me too. We'll just happen to stop there on the way home."

Amanda lifted her head as if she'd heard something. Her hair whipped around as she turned to look down the hall. "Uh-oh," she said.

All at once, Finn felt a numbing coldness pass through him, a wave of nausea, as if all the blood had suddenly drained out of him. He sank to his knees.

Amanda caught him as he was going down. Her books spilled. Some kids stepped out of her way.

"Finn? Finn? Are you okay?"

"Cold . . ." he managed to explain.

She hugged him, trying to warm him. Finn couldn't keep his teeth from chattering. His whole body was shaking.

Amanda pleaded with him. "Finn . . ." She rubbed his arms. "Think of someplace warm. A beach. A boat. Hot, hot sun . . . It's a hot beach on a summer day."

Finn felt himself warming. The more he thought of the beach, the warmer he felt.

A moment later he felt fine. He leaned away

from her. "Whoa," he said. "That was some kind of strange."

A small group of kids that had gathered moved on. Finn stood up.

"Are you sure you're okay?" she asked.

"Felt like I blew a fuse," he told her. "Thanks for the coaching. Where'd you learn that?"

"So much of that stuff is in our minds," was all she said. She giggled. "I thought you'd fainted."

He said, "You turned . . . just before . . . like you heard something. What was with that?"

"I—" She looked away. She didn't offer an answer.

Now it dawned on him what had just happened.

"*It isn't safe,*'" he mumbled.

Amanda's brow knit in grave concern. The second bell rang.

Finn whispered dryly, "Now I know I've got to get to Willa and Maybeck. I'll meet you out by the bikes after the last bell."

Crazy Glaze was crowded with mothers and their children busily painting blank pottery at brightly lit tables. There were several connected rooms, all filled with color and the murmur of activity.

Finn and Amanda locked their bikes out front. Once inside, they were directed to a heavyset gray-haired African American woman who wore hoop earrings and dark purple eye shadow.

"I'm looking for Donnie Maybeck," Finn said.

"You mean Terry," she said, a smile overcoming her. "Donnie's his stage name. Say, aren't you a sweet-looking girl," she said, noticing Amanda and studying her features.

"Who should I say is calling? Wait a minute!" she interrupted herself. "Don't I know you?" she asked Finn. "You're a host, right? I saw you at MGM, during the film shoot."

"Yes, ma'am."

She nodded, proud of herself. "That's it exactly. I was over there nearly every day you all were shooting. But you, girl. I'd remember you, and I don't believe we've met."

"Amanda. A friend of Finn's."

"Well, I'm pleased to meet you both. I'm Terry's Aunt Bess. I run this place. Own it too!" As she grinned, the room seemed a bit brighter. "Kids around here call me Jelly."

"Jelly?" Amanda said.

"It's a long story. It started with jelly donuts, and got out of control from there. Don't ask me!"

"Is Terry around?" Finn asked.

"Terry's out back. But he's taking it easy today. Not feeling exactly top-notch. I'm not sure this is the best day for a visit."

"He didn't happen to feel faint, did he?" Finn blurted out.

The woman's face hardened. She crossed her arms tightly and looked down at Finn. "Now why would you go and ask that?"

"I think I need to see him, Ms. . . . Jelly." Finn saw the way his guess had struck her.

"School nurse said there's a bug going around," she said.

"And maybe that's all it is," Finn said.

"What is it you're not telling me, son?" Jelly asked.

"I really need to see him," Finn pleaded.

When she nodded, her double chin turned into a triple. "Okay. Just not too long. Hear?"

"You!" Maybeck said to Finn, looking up. He was a head taller than either of them. His expression was defiant; there was a hardness in his eyes. He was in the midst of unpacking unglazed ceramics. He didn't want them there.

Finn introduced Amanda.

Maybeck said "Hey" to her. He looked at Finn curiously. "So what's going on?"

"Are we okay to talk here?" Finn asked.

Maybeck looked around, closed a door that led into the front of the shop and said, "We're good."

"How's your sleep these past couple nights?"

"What's with that?" Maybeck asked.

"Had any vivid dreams?"

Maybeck looked searchingly from Finn to Amanda.

Finn said, "She knows. I've told her everything."

"I'm not saying I have or haven't," Maybeck said.

"Did you make these?" Amanda pointed to a series of beautifully painted water pitchers on a shelf amid dozens of other bowls and mugs. The image on the pitchers was the Cinderella Castle.

"Tourists like them."

"But you painted them," she said.

"Yeah. I sell them on the side." He lowered his voice and said to Finn, "Listen, the money . . . from Disney

. . . being a DHI. It's made a big difference for us—my aunt and me—and I can't risk their asking for that money back."

"That's not going to happen."

"How do you know it won't?"

Finn hadn't ever considered such a thing. His mother would kill him if he lost his college money.

"Do you have Internet access?" Amanda asked.

Finn glanced over at her. Why did she always have the best ideas? he wondered.

"Sure," Maybeck answered.

Finn said, "The others and I . . . Tonight we're meeting in my guest room in the Virtual Magic Kingdom Web site to get this stuff straight." He paused and added, "It's happening to all of us, Maybeck. The dreams . . . of being there. The fainting this afternoon."

"Not me." Maybeck looked briefly afraid.

Finn said, "The old guy, Wayne? He's got some kind of mission for us. As a team, I'm talking about. He says we've got to go to sleep at some point, and that when we do, we're going to cross over."

Maybeck looked completely serious. There was not a laughing bone in his body. "I can't mess things up for my aunt."

"We can't stop this," Finn warned. "Whatever's

happening, we can't stop it. At least I haven't been able to. Have you?" He felt another little chill. He said, "It isn't safe."

Maybeck met eyes with him, a mean look, both angry and afraid. He'd heard those words before.

"No way . . ." he said darkly.

"Way," said Finn.

Maybeck said, "Yeah, well . . . then I guess we gotta do this."

Finn's mother fumbled around with the serving plates, as nervous as could be. Her son had never brought a girl home for dinner before, and she was quite beside herself.

She served meat loaf, with green beans and bacon, salad, and cornbread, only to discover that Amanda was a vegetarian.

Finn's father was quieter than usual. About halfway through the meal he asked Amanda to pass the salt.

Finn's mom told his father, "Amanda and Finn are going to chat online together after dinner."

"Is that right?" he asked.

Mr. Whitman challenged their guest. "I don't see why you have to go online to talk. Why can't you just talk if you want to talk?"

"We don't own a computer," Amanda answered. "Or a TV."

Mr. Whitman looked up from his plate, possibly for the first time. "Well, good for you," he said. "Nothing wrong with that. Finn spends way too much time on his, as far as I'm concerned."

"Donald!" Finn's mother snapped at him.

"I'm just making conversation," Mr. Whitman complained.

"Hey, Dad," Finn said, trying to salvage things. "You know that hurricane—I forget its name—the one that turned out in the ocean and came back ashore?"

"Gary."

"Yeah, Gary. Is it true it lost a lot of its power after it went over us?"

"Over half its wind speed. Yes. Downgraded to a tropical storm. But that's pretty typical when storms pass over land. Why?"

"Oh, nothing. Never mind," Finn said.

He glanced at Amanda. She nodded toward her watch.

"We're gonna go up now," Finn said. His parents looked at each other but said nothing.

On their way up the stairs Finn heard his father say, "If those pants of hers get any lower, they'll fall off."

"They *all* wear them that way, dear," Mrs. Whitman said. "She's adorable." She'd lowered her voice to a whisper, but Finn had stopped on the stairs in time to hear.

"Nothing wrong with him having a new friend. He can't spend all his time with Dillard."

His mother then called out loudly, "Leave the bedroom door open, please, Finn."

"I will!" Finn called back.

He gave Amanda his chair in front of the screen. He sat on a wooden chest that he dragged from his closet. It contained an old model train set.

"Five minutes to seven," Amanda said, checking her watch.

Finn entered the Virtual Magic Kingdom Web site. He logged on, selected GUEST ROOMS from the map of the Magic Kingdom, and then the option of picking a room from an alphabetical list. He located FINN'S ROOM and double-clicked.

The screen went black. Some music played. His room appeared.

It was a stone room, as if they were in a dungeon or castle. Using credit he'd earned by winning challenges on the site, he'd furnished the room with a pair of lime-green couches, two chairs, a soda machine, and three posters on the walls.

"What's with the color of those couches?" Amanda asked.

"What? I like them."

"Trust me, you're color-blind."

Finn's character was an illustrated boy who wore brightly colored jams and a light-blue T-shirt. Finn used the mouse to move his character across the screen, get a soda from the machine, and return to one of the two chairs. The small figure sat down and waited, occasionally raising his arm, under Finn's direction, to lift the can to his face.

"This is wild," Amanda said.

"Have you never seen VMK?" he asked. "Everyone at school's on here twenty-four seven."

A few minutes after seven, a second figure, a girl, appeared in the room. She wore hip huggers and a lemon-yellow top that showed her stomach.

A dialogue bubble appeared above her. **Angelface 13**, it read.

Cool room appeared inside the bubble.

Finn: Thnx, said the bubble above the boy in the chair. **Grab a soda.**

The girl character bought herself a drink and took a seat on the couch near Finn.

Angelface 13: U got any tunes?

Finn: Yeah, but we're going 2 chat. Let's hang.

Others coming soon.

"It's Charlene," Amanda said out loud. "I can tell by the way she dresses."

"Yeah," Finn said, agreeing.

Willa and Philby's characters appeared almost simultaneously. Philby, with red hair. Willa, dressed like a hippie. They too got drinks and gathered by the others, both standing. Philby (**philitup**) complimented Finn on his choice of posters, clearly impressed that Finn had earned enough credits—"creds"—to purchase them. Willa chatted with Charlene about some new clothes that she'd found in one of the merchandise stores.

"This is a really weird thing to say," Amanda said, "but I feel like I'm in the room, not just watching."

"I know," Finn said. "It's highly addictive." He added, "I'd make you a character, but for now I'm not sure the others should know you're listening."

"No, no! I agree. I don't want them to know. I don't want to be seen as a problem."

"You're not a problem!" Finn said, thinking he should go ahead and register a character for her. "Far from it. Without you, this meeting wouldn't be happening."

Dilltoast showed up in the room and asked, **What's up?**

"That's my friend, Dillard."

"We met," Amanda said.

Finn's character stood and led Dillard's into the far corner of the room to talk to him. Finn explained to Amanda, "You have to be near each other to talk. It's called proximity, for obvious reasons. Dill and I can talk over here, and the others won't see it and . . ."

His explanation was made clear as Charlene and Willa continued talking, presumably about clothes, but the dialogue in their bubbles was replaced with exclamation points, dollar signs, and ampersands—unreadable gibberish.

Finn tried to politely ask Dillard to go away. Dillard didn't get the idea at first and forced Finn to get a little blunt once Maybeck arrived. "That didn't go so hot," he told Amanda as Dillard's character left the room.

"Tell him about it tomorrow in person. If you make it into something secret, that you're sharing, he won't even remember this."

"Good with people are you?" Finn thought about this: she was good with people. For one thing, she'd survived his dad at the dinner table.

Maybeck passed on the offer of a drink. He'd given his character a sizable Afro, blue jeans, and a white T-shirt. Somehow it made him look taller than the others, which he was in person as well.

Mybest: Let's do this. I got homework.

Finn: Okay. We're all here.

Each of the others said hello. Then Finn continued.

Finn: we've all had basically the same "dream" or we wouldn't be here. Maybeck and I both felt kinda sick, like fainting, earlier today. anybody else?

The dialogue bubble above Willa's character started "talking."

willatree: yes. I felt awful, but only for a few minutes.

angelface 13: me too

philitup: yup

Mybest: so what's with that?

Finn: they aren't dreams. charlene and philby and I were all in the park last night. I got burned on the arm. when I woke up, I had the same burn on the same arm. it's for real. It wasn't a dream.

Maybeck's character moved around the room but stayed close enough to chat. Willa got up off the couch and moved over next to Charlene. No writing appeared above any of the characters.

Amanda said, "I think you freaked them out."

Finn complained, "What was I supposed to do?"

angelface 13: I saw him get burned. It's for real.

philitup: what's weird is that over there we look like our DHIs, but Finn getting burned means we must be part

Finn: human. Part DHI, part human. That's what Wayne, the old guy, said we were.

Mybest: does anyone hear how completely stupid this sounds?

philitup: we all got sick at basically the same moment. That may sound stupid, but it felt awful.

Mybest: so what we do?

Amanda, looking on, said, "Now, Finn. You've got to tell them now."

Finn: if we all go to bed—to sleep—at the same time tonight, maybe we'll arrive there together.

Mybest: tell me you're kidding?

Finn: That's the way it works. i'm sure of it. Wayne wants us all there at the same time.

Finn felt a rush of heat: all five of them had crossed over at various times. They all shared this same experience. His fingers hovered above the keyboard.

Finn: the only way we're gonna know what's up is to go to bed at the same time and hope we wake up over there 2gether. tonight. K?

One by one, the characters answered.

willatree: I'll be there.

angelface 13: I'm having trouble falling asleep, but I'll try.

philitup: I'm there.

Mybest: word.

Finn's character stood up from the couch. He went to the corner and dropped the can into an open box—his makeshift trash can. Charlene followed his lead and did the same.

Mybest: we all play VMK, right? What if that's got something to do with it?

He had a point, Finn thought. The game had an otherworldly quality.

Finn: we've got to talk to Wayne. How about 9:00 tonight?

Each of the characters agreed to the time, a text bubble appearing above their heads. Then, one by one, they checked out. Finn's character stood alone in the empty room.

"You look kinda lonely just standing there," Amanda said.

"I think I'm afraid," Finn admitted. He couldn't believe he'd said that aloud.

"I bet they all are too," Amanda said. "Remember that fear is a human emotion. A DHI wouldn't feel fear."

The way she said it, so calm, and like she knew what she was talking about—really *knew* it—gave Finn this strange tingling feeling. He thought how strange it was that Amanda had just showed up the way she had, become his friend right as he began crossing over. How could he ask for a better friend? And yet . . . Was there something she wasn't telling him?

He caught a look in her eye as if she'd said too much and now regretted it. She looked away, breaking their eye contact.

"Finn?" It was his mother calling from downstairs.

It disturbed the moment. Finn didn't ask Amanda anything—but he'd wanted to.

He checked the time. It was going on eight o'clock.

"I can drive Amanda home now," she hollered upstairs.

"I wish I could go," Amanda said. She didn't mean home.

"Yeah, that would be cool." He caught himself using that word again. She'd teased him about it earlier, but not now.

"It'll be all right," she said, standing. "Remember everything so you can tell me."

He walked her downstairs to the door, where his mother was waiting with a smile. The three of them walked out to the driveway. Finn took the backseat. Amanda and his mom talked about boring girl stuff: favorite shopping malls and places to get your hair cut.

She lived on the far edge of their school district, in what had once been a small church. There was a stained-glass window in the center of the roof's peak: a blue background with a white angel. Lit from inside, it looked as if the angel were flying. He didn't know why, but it seemed appropriate for Amanda.

Finn hurried his mother to drive faster on the way back home.

She looked at him funny when he told her he was going to be late to bed.

It was like something from Star Trek, or Power Rangers, Finn thought. He was standing at Central Plaza, a circle of grass and sidewalks in front of the castle. Over the next several minutes, one by one, the other four DHIs appeared. Charlene first, lying on the grass to his left, wearing her nightgown. She stretched her arms as if waking up. Philby was next—his red hair electric as a DHI. He came hurrying in from Tomorrowland. Willa showed up on the road to Finn's right. She also wore pajamas—shorts and a matching T-shirt.

Maybeck came walking up Main Street alongside Wayne, who drove a Disney golf cart.

"Well, well," Wayne said. "The gang's all here." He climbed out of the cart and made a point of saying hello to Willa, whom he'd only met once before.

A loud crashing noise came from somewhere in Tomorrowland. Cheering followed this.

"Something wild's going on over there," Finn said, pointing.

A concerned Wayne said quickly, "Follow me! And not a word until I say."

They followed Wayne and his cart up the ramp that

led into the enormous castle. Finn noted that the DHIs glowed and shimmered once inside the shadow of the castle arches.

"Memorize all this carefully!" Wayne called back to the DHIs.

He led them through a gift shop and into a storage room, then through a heavy medieval-style door that he unlocked with a large key, and down a nondescript hall, through another door, and into a vast, cavernous space.

Finn stopped. Staircases led in every direction, interconnecting in impossible ways, some upside down. A variety of oddly shaped doors of all sizes faced him at every level. Each corridor and staircase connected to the next in the most unlikely, impossible ways. All interlocked. It was a giant puzzle that somehow all fit together. And yet it made no sense: inverted stairs?

"We call this Escher's Keep. Walt admired M. C. Escher's work," Wayne said, climbing a staircase.

"Who's Escher?" Finn asked.

"Do your homework," Wayne admonished. "The keep was built as part of an Alice in Wonderland attraction. But it never opened."

"Why not?"

"Walt decided to keep it for himself."

Finn reached the top of some steep stairs, out of

breath. He continued down a darkened hall and looked up to see Wayne standing *upside down* on a landing a few yards ahead.

Wayne said, "Don't be fooled. You're fine. But a single misstep and you'll end up in a slide that will dump you into the moat. So stay to the left, and only step on the blue tiles, never the white or the red. Pass it along to the others."

Finn repeated the weird instructions in a whisper. A moment later he stood with Wayne. To the others, now arriving, both Wayne and Finn appeared to be standing upside down.

He heard Maybeck say, "Okay! This is way cool."

Wayne said, "This is a good place to come if you're ever in trouble or trying to hide. Without a guide to show the way, no one makes it up the first time. Memorize it carefully. The castle has several secret entrances. I'll show you if we have time. Once in here, you're safe."

It isn't safe, Finn remembered Charlene saying. He wasn't sure he wanted to go any farther.

Wayne continued, "The other place you should be safe is if you follow the tracks out of the Frontierland train station toward the Indian Encampment. There are some teepees out there that aren't programmed for DHI projection."

"Safe from what?" Finn asked.

"Ah!" Wayne said, ignoring Finn's question. "Here come the others. Follow me! Memorize!" he reminded. "The next two staircases are fakes."

Finn was stunned by how incredibly real each of the many staircases appeared. The first staircase turned out to be nothing but paint on a wall. Wayne led him to the real staircase and together they climbed it.

Finn looked back, carefully committing the route to memory. He called ahead to Wayne. "If I'm half holo-gram, half human, as you said, how can I touch any-thing? Shouldn't I only half touch it?"

"Have you studied Einstein, Finn?" Finn didn't want to sound dumb, so he didn't answer. "It's time you did. There's more space between atoms than there are atoms. And yet atoms hold together somehow and form what we think of as a solid. We can touch, smell, taste. It all comes down to what you believe. What you think you can do."

The only thing Finn knew about Einstein had to do with bagels. He stuck to more practical matters. "How will we ever get back down?"

As he reached yet another landing, Finn realized Wayne was nowhere to be seen.

"Take the middle door," Wayne's voice instructed.

Finn faced half of a hexagon: three doors, all at angles. He walked through the middle door, which sprang shut behind him. He now stood in a pitch-black space. Being part hologram, Finn glowed, casting a bluish light into the absolute blackness. But the space seemed to swallow his light, to go on forever. He saw nothing.

Charlene came in next. Even when the door opened, Finn saw no walls, only blackness.

"I don't exactly love this," Charlene said, a pulsing blue light in the dark.

The way her voice sounded—so close and bright—told Finn that they were in a very small room.

"Look up," he said.

"Are those stars for real?" Charlene asked.

"Is anything real here?"

The door opened. Philby, Willa, and Maybeck entered. As the door shut, the stars reappeared.

"Wow!" Philby said.

"Yeah," Finn agreed.

"What's this about?" Maybeck asked.

Finn jumped as Wayne said from behind him, "Move to the center, everyone." He'd been standing there all along.

The kids crowded together into a group. Finn felt the old man's hand grab his wrist and pull him toward what turned out to be a wall.

"Feel this?" Wayne asked.

"Yes." It was a smooth, glassy button.

"And this?"

Another.

"Yes."

"Push."

Finn pushed. The floor vibrated and the stars grew closer.

It took a moment, but Willa understood before the others. "It's an elevator!"

"An elevator without walls," Finn said, for it wasn't the floor that appeared to be moving, but the walls.

"It's an elevator *floor*," Maybeck said. "A platform."

The overhead constellations grew closer. As they reached the Big Dipper, Finn could imagine it as a cleverly shaped door.

"You gotta love this," Philby said.

"I don't have to," Charlene protested, sounding a little frightened.

The floor stopped. Finn heard a click. He pushed against the wall—the Big Dipper—and it opened.

They entered a small apartment, full of old furniture in pastel colors, like something from Finn's grandparents' house. A small drafting table occupied the far corner. Most of one wall was filled with books. A tiny galley kitchen was next to the room's only window.

Narrow and small, the slit window belonged in a castle. It was tinted with a blue theatrical lighting gel with a tiny hole cut into it to allow you to peer outside. Finn looked down over the entire Magic Kingdom. The view took his breath away. They were *very* high up.

"Welcome to Walt's secret hideaway," Wayne said.

Three phones hung from the wall: red, blue, and yellow. Philby studied them.

"Never touch any of those," Wayne advised, eyeing each of the kids.

Charlene peered out the small hole in the window. "Beautiful," she said. That led to each of the kids taking a turn, oohing and ahhing.

Wayne waited for them to face him. It was a small apartment with barely enough room for the six of them.

"You were each picked for a reason, or you wouldn't be here," he said. "Our selection of the DHIs was careful to the point of painstaking. We've brought you here to help us. I'm going to share a story with you. A fable. It's something that has been in my care a long, long time. Walt entrusted me with this, and it has been in my head ever since. All fables have names. This one is called The Stonecutter and, as it turns out, has been around a few thousand years. But take note: Walt called it The Stonecutter's Quill. It's up to you to find out why he added *quill* to the name. But here's the story. I believe it to be the key to stopping the forces that are gathering."

The kids looked for places to sit. Willa took a chair. Charlene and Philby the couch. Maybeck sat on the floor. Finn stood.

No one said a word. Wayne had their full attention.

"It was a hot, sweltering day, and the stonecutter balanced on his haunches, chisel and hammer in hand, streams of sweat running down his back as he broke bits of rock away from the base of a wall of stone. It was hard, blistering work, and it felt like the sun had no mercy on him.

"How wonderful it must be to have the power of the sun, he thought. If I were the sun, no one could resist me! I wish I were the sun!

"In an instant, he found himself looking down on the earth, beating on it with his heat and energy. He was the sun, and he liked the way he touched everything and everyone below him without mercy. In his presence, people would be thirsty, they would be hot, and they would always know he was there.

"Suddenly, he realized that there was something impeding him. He could not touch the earth with his power. He looked down and saw that a cloud had interposed itself between him and the earth.

"Hmm, he thought. In spite of my great power,

there is something that thwarts me. Surely this cloud is mightier than I am. I wish I were the cloud!

"And in an instant, he found he was the cloud, and he could block the sun all day long. What's more, he could rain on those below him, bringing cold, eroding buildings, drowning what he pleased. Surely there was nothing more powerful than he was now!

"But he felt himself being swayed, and quite without his consent, he was being pushed and he could not resist the movement. He found that the wind was blowing him to the side, and he saw that because he could not defy it, it was mightier than him. How I wish I were the wind! he thought.

"And he was. Where he blew, huge trees bent. He could push great walls of water where he pleased. He could topple the tallest, most majestic buildings. Surely he was all-powerful now.

"But as he swept across the world, he came across something that stopped him. He looked and realized that the mountain before him could not be penetrated. As hard as he might blow against it, he could not push it to the side. Look how it resists me! he thought. Surely this mountain is mightier than me. I wish I were the mountain!

"And he was. He sat, imperial and bold, tall and proud, bolted to the earth, and he knew that there was nothing in all the world that could move him, could destroy him, or could overcome him. He was the mightiest thing of all.

"But then he realized something. From somewhere far below, he felt he was being reduced. He was being destroyed—torn apart—quite against his wishes, and he could do nothing about it. What is there mightier than a mountain? he asked himself. Not the sun, the cloud, or the wind . . . What could it be?

"With great effort, he looked down, and there, far below, at his very base . . .

"He saw a stonecutter."

The kids said nothing, focused on Wayne expectantly.

Wayne said, "The things in the story you need to focus on are the *sun, cloud, wind, and stone.* At least we're pretty sure about that. Note the order. All four of these themes are seen repeatedly in the Magic Kingdom. Somehow they are meant to lead us to a solution, a way to defeat the darker powers that have begun to threaten the park."

Silence.

"Comments?" Wayne asked, reminding Finn of an English teacher.

"Be careful what you wish for. That's the theme, isn't it?" Maybeck asked.

Finn said, "It also says to be satisfied with who you are."

"Not to mention that no matter how strong you think you are, there's always something stronger," Willa contributed.

Philby said, "So it's about power. It's a study of power."

"Walt told me that story," Wayne explained, "and then said something I will never forget. He said, 'I have plans for this place that should put things in perspective, Wayne.' And there was this twinkle in his eye. There was something more to it than he was letting on. At least that's been my opinion all these years."

"But what?" Finn asked.

Wayne shrugged. He repeated: "I have plans for this place that should put things in perspective."

"And we're supposed to figure out why he called it 'The Stonecutter's Quill'?" Willa asked.

"Yes, it's up to the five of you to solve the fable. Others have tried before you, myself included, but to no avail. As matters grew more urgent, we came up with the idea of the DHIs. You have one foot in the character world, one in the real. We need not only to solve whatever the fable is supposed to tell us, but we need to apprehend and stop the Overtakers responsible for our recent problems."

"And we're the chosen ones," Maybeck said skeptically.

"Indeed, you are. Very carefully chosen, at that: intelligence, athleticism, artistry, computer knowledge."

"What if we don't want to be chosen?" Willa asked.

Finn answered. "There's not much choice. We're going to cross over when we go to sleep."

"But that must be your doing," Willa said to Wayne accusingly.

The old man looked back impassively. For a moment it seemed he might refuse to answer. Then he said, "It's out of my hands now." He raised his arms dramatically. "I've waited a long time to tell that story to you."

Willa spoke, "What are we up against?"

Wayne said, "You know how you can sometimes sense a storm before it ever rains? You can almost smell it? Whatever is happening to this place is like that: we know it's coming. Bad things have been happening, but worse things are on their way. We're powerless to do anything about them. You are not. You five can change it."

Maybeck snorted.

Philby, deep in thought, complained. "What if there isn't enough time?"

He won Wayne's attention.

Finn explained, "This afternoon we all . . . kind of fainted. All of us. Right at the same time, and all in completely different locations."

Wayne's face wrinkled in concern. He considered this carefully and said, "Was this sometime after two o'clock?"

Finn gasped. "How would you know that?"

"The DHIs here in the park—they went down for a few minutes this afternoon. Something to do with the computer server. Maybeck?"

Maybeck shied from the summons.

"That's right," Philby said, remembering. "You're a computer freak, aren't you, Maybeck?"

"Freak? I'm freaking good with them, if that's what you're asking."

Finn speculated, "If we're able to cross over at night—and we certainly are, then maybe if something happens to the DHIs during the day, it also happens to us."

Wayne said, "I think you'd better hurry." He pursed his lips and looked each of them in the eyes before saying, "Once the Overtakers realize you intend to help us—that you're here to stop them—I believe they'll do whatever they can to stop you first. Maybe your fainting is the result of their dark powers. If they can stop you from crossing over, we're defeated. Fear is one way to stop you." He paused a moment and said, "This is new ground for *all* of us."

Finn felt a chill run up his spine.

Still deep in concentration, Philby said, "Walt was an artist. An animator. He drew things. You draw things with pencils and pens. *Quills.*"

"Yes," Wayne agreed. "We got that far as well."

"So the solution to the fable has something to do with that," Philby said. "A pen. A pencil. A quill."

Wayne nodded. "Just as we've thought these many years. But what it is exactly, and where to find it? We have no idea."

Willa had her own concerns. "What do you mean by 'dark powers'? Some kind of magic?"

"What puts us in a bad mood when just a minute before we felt so good?" Wayne asked. "What makes us afraid of the dark when we know perfectly well there's nothing bad out there? What explains that sometimes we think of a person and two seconds later the phone rings, and it's that same person calling us?" Again, Wayne looked at the kids one by one, his face deadly serious. "Not all such forces have to do with hats and rabbits. There are forces bigger than all of us. Good, and bad."

Wayne reached toward the wall. "Good luck," he said as he pushed a circular metal plate embossed with a silhouette of Mickey Mouse. A panel in the floor opened up beneath him. Wayne fell through and disappeared.

Finn jumped up, ahead of the others. The floor was solid again. Wayne was gone.

Sitting on the coffee table in the center of the room was what looked like a small black garage-door opener with a single red button.

Wayne had used it to send him back to his bed on his earlier visits. Finn pointed it out for the others to see. "Well, I guess that's it. So who's in? Who's up for solving the Stonecutter fable?"

One by one, the other DHIs tentatively lifted their hands. They had accepted Wayne's challenge.

He said, "Philby and Willa will work to connect the fable to the Magic Kingdom. There has to be something we're supposed to *do* with the story. Maybeck will find out as much as he can about the DHI servers and what we might do to protect them, to protect us. Charlene and I will study up on Walt Disney—why he might have picked the Stonecutter's fable, what's with the quill, and anything else we can find out. Sound okay?"

No one disagreed. Finn was the acknowledged leader.

Finn said, "I doubt this button is going to cross over with me. It'll remain here."

Maybeck said, "My guess is, it's a proximity thing, like the dialogue bubbles in VMK. You have to be near it when it's pushed in order to go back. So if you're ever in trouble, get up here to this room and push this button."

"Okay?"

Everyone nodded.

Finn indicated the black fob with the red button. They all gathered close together.

Maybeck said, "It might be smart to hold hands."

The kids looked anxiously and apprehensively among themselves.

Finn said, "It wouldn't be good to get left behind."

They grabbed each other's hands immediately, forming a circle. Willa took Finn's right forearm, freeing his hand to reach down and press the button.

The world went dark.

The following night, the five DHIs gathered near the Riverboat Cruise as the first rumblings of a thunderstorm echoed like faraway drums in the distance. The approaching clouds drew a veil across the night sky. The river's black water swirled and lapped lazily at the riverbank. Wayne had mentioned the Indian Encampment as a safe location, and this had led the DHIs to meet here.

The cluster of extremely realistic-looking teepees sat atop a rise, overlooking Tom Sawyer Island. The encampment included a dozen human-size models of Native Americans doing a day's work: chopping wood, tending a fire. At the fake campfire, an old Native American woman squatted while she cooked.

As Finn led the DHIs inside the first of the teepees, they all disappeared. Charlene gasped aloud. "We're ..."

"Invisible," Maybeck answered. "Our holograms are not projected inside the teepees. Basically, we're in a kind of hologram-projection shadow here."

Finn said, "That's got to be why Wayne suggested it. It's the perfect hiding place."

"Our holograms apparently have been programmed to project inside most attractions," Maybeck said.

Philby said, "The plan was to have us guide guests onto the rides at some point. Still is. Sit there with them and explain the history of the attraction. That producer Brad told me about it when we were all at MGM."

Finn said, "But here, we're safe."

The small space was crowded with the five of them. Maybeck's crossed legs—and *only* his legs—showed because they were near the teepee's open door. A part of Charlene's left knee showed as well.

"This is too weird," said an invisible Willa.

Maybeck raised and lowered his arm into the light that came through the door, making his hand appear and disappear. He said, "It's like cell phone reception in a tunnel."

"Let's not forget," Philby pointed out in a whisper, "that though we may be invisible, we can hear each other. That means we can also *be heard*."

"Good point," Willa whispered back.

Finn also spoke quietly. "So, where are we? Willa? Philby?"

Philby said, "The Stonecutter fable is supposed to lead us to a quill: maybe a special pen or pencil; maybe something used by Walt Disney a long time ago. Our

121

clues are: sun, cloud, wind, and stone. As Wayne said, they're found all over in the park."

"The attractions," Willa said. "Walt knew they would stay behind long after he was gone."

, Philby said, "Rides dealing with sun, clouds, wind, and stone."

"We're working on which attractions have to do with each clue," Willa said.

Finn pointed out, "But Walt died before the park was ever open, didn't he? So he wouldn't have known what attractions would end up getting built. Not all of them, anyway. Maybe we're supposed to try to solve this in Disneyland, not here."

Willa said, "But he had dozens of loyal people working for him. His brother. His nephew. He could have passed his wishes along to any one of them."

Philby added, "And Wayne worked here, in Disney World. Walt told the fable to Wayne, and no one else."

"That we know of," Willa reminded.

"The answers are here," Philby said convincingly. "We just have to put it all together."

Finn asked Maybeck if he'd found out anything about the DHI servers. Any clue as to why they all fainted at the same time. "Was Wayne right about that?"

"You remember we had to sign those releases *before*

they started turning us into DHIs?" Maybeck replied. "Some of these imaging techniques have never been tried before. That's what makes it look so cool, right? It's, like, totally new stuff. The DHI servers clearly control our holograms, but why they could affect us as humans is really weird. In crossing back over we must take something of our DHIs with us. We don't see it, we don't feel it, but it's there. That might explain how messing with the servers made us feel faint. I don't know about the rest of you, but I'm not real keen on someone else controlling me. I'm not loving that idea. I think the time will come when we'd rather have control of the servers ourselves. So that's what I'm working on."

Murmurs rippled through the group. No one objected to the idea of gaining self-control.

"The Fall Games are tomorrow," Charlene said. "Is everyone here going?"

They realized they would all be there, participating in various sports.

"That gives us a chance to meet again," Finn said. "Let's meet by the snack bar before any of the sports get going."

"Psst!" Maybeck's arm appeared briefly as he reached across the doorway and pulled Charlene's knee back inside. In the shadow her leg became invisible.

Finn then heard what Maybeck had heard: the

sound of footsteps, the crunching of gravel. Nearby. Security guards? At the same time, he felt a sudden draft, like when he stepped into an air-conditioned room. He shivered.

"I feel you . . ." It was a woman's hoarse whisper, raspy and dry, as if she had sand in her throat. Gooseflesh rippled up Finn's arms and down his spine. He was *freezing* now. "You don't belong here. Go away."

The sound of footsteps moved slowly away from their teepee, and continued on to the next. Finn held his breath. The sound stopped, and then headed back toward them.

Inside the teepee came a soft shuffling sound as the invisible Maybeck and Charlene moved farther away from the door.

"I feel you," came that awful voice again. "You can't hide from me."

It wasn't just any woman's voice. Finn had heard that voice before. But how was that possible?

The footfalls circled the teepee and came around front again. Two legs appeared, with black stockings that ended at low-heeled, shiny black shoes. An invisible Willa reached over and found Finn's hand and clutched it tightly. Hers was warm and clammy.

The black-stockinged legs bent as a hand appeared in the teepee's doorway.

A green hand. The hand emerged from the end of a long black sleeve. Green as a lizard, the knuckles bent and bumpy, the nails as long as claws. Charlene gasped aloud. Too loud.

The air grew colder still. The woman bent over fully and peered into the dark teepee. She wore a robelike black dress with jagged purple fringe and a purple stripe running up the middle—some kind of costume.

"Interesting," she said, staring into an empty teepee.

Now Finn understood how he knew this voice: it was from one of the Disney movies. But which one?

He racked his brain, as Willa's hand grew colder in his. She squeezed so hard, it hurt.

The woman bent lower, and lower still. The air grew colder and colder.

A green neck appeared, then a green chin, a green nose, and finally her full face. Wretched, yet somehow beautiful.

It was Maleficent, the mean-spirited witch from *Sleeping Beauty*, the most ill-tempered and dreaded witch of all.

His eyes were stinging with ice, Finn looked away, thinking the cold might kill him. When he looked back, she was gone. Two footprint-shaped patches of ice showed where her shoes had been. The ground was *frozen solid* where she had stood.

No one spoke for several long minutes. Finn was the first to break the silence, in a faint whisper. "Was that an illusion?"

"If it was, it was one solid illusion," Maybeck said.

Philby asked. "What about the cold? Was I the only one who felt that?"

"No way!" they all chorused.

"I had my eyes shut," Charlene confessed.

"Me too," Willa admitted. Only then did she let go of Finn's hand. He was glad they were all invisible. He wouldn't have wanted to explain their holding hands.

Maybeck scooted forward, and as he did, partially reappeared at the mouth of the teepee's open door. About a third of him peered outside, the rest of him invisible.

"She's gone," Maybeck said.

"She?" Charlene asked.

"Her skin certainly looked real enough," Finn said.

"That was green *skin*, not green makeup. Mark my words," Maybeck said, "I know the difference."

"Are you suggesting what I think you're suggesting?" Willa asked.

Finn offered the only explanation he could think of: "I think we just met an Overtaker."

The Wide World of Sports complex housed eleven baseball diamonds, a separate major- and minor-league baseball stadium with seating for nine thousand, five sports fields, a tennis complex, and a 400-meter running track. The facility had as many parking lots as an airport. Various buildings, all painted yellow, were scattered around the grounds and housed a café, locker rooms, and meeting halls.

On this October afternoon, nearly a thousand local students and their families jammed the complex for the annual Fall Games.

"You're not telling me anything," Amanda complained, as she and Finn walked toward the snack bar. "All you care about is hooking up with the others. What, I'm suddenly not your friend?"

"It's not like that."

"Looks that way to me."

"Listen . . . all sorts of weird stuff's happening."

"Well, that certainly clarifies things."

"It's complicated." Suddenly Finn spotted Philby and Maybeck, both in their gym clothes, as they climbed the steps to the central facility that housed locker rooms and an indoor-outdoor snack bar. A TV news crew was picking out kids to interview. Finn steered well clear of the cameras; his celebrity as a DHI made him a prime target for TV.

Finn felt the curious warmth on the back of his neck that he always felt when someone's eyes were on him. Through the chaotic crowds of kids and parents, coaches and referees, volunteers and Wide World employees, Finn spotted a girl looking at him. Not just any girl. She was beautiful, with pale skin that set off her jet-black hair. Her deep-set gray eyes captivated him, even from a distance. He'd never seen her before.

It didn't take Amanda long to notice Finn gazing at the girl. She stared long and hard at her.

"Who's that?" Finn asked.

"Who?" Amanda tried to pretend she hadn't seen her.

"The girl you're staring at."

"Never seen her before." Is Amanda upset with me? Finn wondered. She turned and hurried off.

Finn called out to stop her, but she pretended not to hear.

The pale girl with the black hair smiled at Finn, who couldn't avoid passing next to her on his way to join the others.

"Hey, Finn," she said, as if they knew each other.

He stopped. "Hey."

"I'm Jez."

"That's an unusual name."

"Short for Jezebel. It's from the Bible." She wasn't proud of this. "My mother. You know how that goes."

"Lawrence Finnegan Whitman. My parents actually thought they'd call me Larry. Larry! Can you imagine? I switched it to Finn in third grade, though it's not much better." He couldn't stop his mouth from talking. He told himself, *Shut up!*, but he kept on going. "And then all the fish jokes started coming. Fin, this. Fin, that."

"What's your sport?"

It was as if she hadn't heard him. He felt relieved. "Soccer. Yours?"

"Spectator. I came to watch."

Her eyes were gray with green specks, like imperfect jewels.

"Have we met?" he asked.

"I don't think so."

"But you knew my name."

"I know all about you." The way she said it bothered Finn. "Because of the Magic Kingdom!" she explained. "You're my favorite Disney host."

Finn felt awkward and uncomfortable. What was

he supposed to say to that? He was saved by the public address system. Players were supposed to find their teams. Finn wanted to catch up with his fellow DHIs.

"Well," he said, "I gotta go."

"There's a Girl Scout car wash tomorrow," she said casually, like an afterthought. When she laughed, it sounded almost—musical. "You could come by if you want."

"Yeah . . . maybe . . ."

"It's at Dangerous Dan's."

Finn hurried up the stairs and past the snack bar.

He found the others in a sour-smelling locker room marked VISITORS B. Backpacks, athletic bags, and smelly shoes surrounded them. Finn and Maybeck organized plastic chairs into a circle.

Philby said, "Willa and I have made some progress."

Finn felt a wrenching in his gut. The deeper they went, the more he feared they were in danger.

Philby glanced toward the door. Now Finn did too, because, like Philby, he thought he felt something coming from there: a slight chill. A familiar chill.

"Are we going to talk about last night?" Charlene asked, clearly unsettled.

"What's to talk about?" Maybeck said. "We were

130

visited by Maleficent, a witch with green skin and black tights, who brought the ambient temperature down to about five below zero." He spoke with so much sarcasm that no one dared bring the subject up again.

Finn told Philby, "The games are starting. We've got to hurry. Have you got anything?"

Philby explained, "The first clue in the fable is sun. There are plenty of suns in the park. But supposedly the ride with the biggest sun is It's a Small World. I think we should start there."

"Start *what*?" Charlene asked.

"Looking for clues."

"What kind of clues?" she persisted.

"I'm not sure we'll know until we find one."

"Does anybody else hear how ridiculous this sounds?" Maybeck asked.

Finn said, "We're going to end up in the park tonight, like it or not. We might as well have a plan."

Willa spoke up. "We should all go to bed early, right at eight, as the park closes. Agreed?"

Maybeck snorted. "You guys are crazy. You know that?"

Finn said, "We need *all of us*, Maybeck." He felt awash with a sudden wave of cold again. Not as strong as at the teepee, but not normal. He lowered his voice. "I think we're done here."

The others suddenly felt the cold as well. Maybeck's smugness fell from his face. He said, "Okay, I'll be there."

"But what about the green—thing, person, woman?" Charlene asked.

Maybeck answered. He'd lost his sarcasm. "Listen, we'd better stay alert. Not only when we're in the park." He added cautiously in a whisper, "Are we so sure this crossing over thing is a one-way street? If we can cross over to there, who says they can't cross over to here?"

15

"Finn, are you sure you feel all right?" his mother said, looking up from the kitchen sink where she was doing dishes. His father hummed as he wiped down the kitchen table.

"I'm fine. I just want to go to bed early, that's all."

"For the third or fourth night in a row," his mother said.

His father barely looked up. "Try to sneak out again, you're grounded for the rest of your life."

Finn and his mother exchanged a look: she'd told his dad, after saying she wouldn't.

"I'm not going to sneak out," Finn promised.

"I'll take away your computer. No more e-mail. No more gaming."

This was the worst threat he could make.

His father looked up. "There was a break-in at a welding shop the other night. A bunch of gear was stolen. Same night, the police—the police, this is—reported a bunch of handcuffs missing from a storage room. This was all over the news. You and your friends go sneaking around at night, and you'll be blamed for things like that, you understand? Whether you had anything to do with them or not. You end up at the wrong place at the wrong time and it's going to look bad—very bad—for you."

"Wouldn't the police have security cameras, Dad?" Finn didn't really want the answer to this, but he had to know. Wayne had mentioned the break-in.

"I don't have any idea! I'm just worried about *you*, Finn, not whatever was stolen. Are you listening to anything I'm saying?"

"Is your homework done?" his mother inquired, changing the subject. She knew when to rescue him.

"All done. Seriously, I'm just *tired*."

"It's because you sleep too much," his father said. "More yard work would be good for you. Why, when I was your age—"

"Dad!" Finn complained. "Can we maybe talk about this in the morning?"

The digital clock that was part of the stove read 7:45. Finn needed to be in bed and asleep by eight if he was to meet the others.

Finn dressed warmly and climbed into bed, boots and all. He pulled the sheet and blanket up high in case his mother looked in on him. She might wake him if she saw he was wearing street clothes. He had no idea what might happen to his DHI if he were rudely awakened from sleep, but he didn't want to find out.

He lay there in bed: 7:55. He didn't feel particularly sleepy. If he didn't cross over, then someone else would have to lead the group. This thought made him more anxious and less sleepy: 8:04. He felt his chances slipping away. How would he find them if he arrived late? The Magic Kingdom was *huge*! This led him to wonder how it was that they all arrived in the same general area. Wayne hadn't explained nearly enough of this.

The front-door chime sounded.

It was an odd time of night for visitors. Their next-door neighbors always used the back door.

"Finn?" his mother called upstairs.

Both annoyed and curious, Finn dragged himself out of bed. He headed to the door and then caught a look at himself in the mirror. He was fully dressed, head to toe, in day clothes that he hadn't been wearing earlier. What would his mother think of that?

He removed his boots and socks and rolled up the legs of his jeans. If he threw a bathrobe over his clothes, he'd look ready for bed.

A glance into the mirror told him he had to lose the jacket, or look like the Incredible Hulk. Checking himself one last time, he headed out into the hall.

Jez stood inside the front door talking to his mother.

Finn felt stupid wearing a bathrobe. Too late. She'd glanced up and seen him.

He summoned his courage and descended, as if it were perfectly normal to be ready for bed at eight o'clock. He felt warm under the robe and layers of clothes.

"Hey, Jez!" A million thoughts ran around in his busy brain. How did she know where he lived? What was she doing here?

He glanced at the grandfather clock: 8:10. This was a *serious* problem.

His mother couldn't shut up, of course. She rambled on about how refreshing it was to meet one of Finn's friends, and such a cute girl at that.

Finn shot her a private look. His mom excused herself to the kitchen.

Jez said, "I came by to congratulate you."

Finn felt confused.

"Soccer," Jez said. "You guys took third."

The clock read 8:12.

"Well," Finn said, moving to open the door, "Thanks a lot. That was really nice of you."

"Nice bathrobe," Jez said, stifling a grin. "You feel okay?"

Truth was, Finn was overheating in all the layers. Sweat trickled off his forehead. He mopped it up with his sleeve.

"Just a little tired. Probably just the game."

She nodded, but studied him oddly. He felt one of his pant legs slip down. He bent over and stuffed it back up, without offering an explanation.

The doorbell rang.

Mrs. Whitman charged out of the kitchen. Finn tried to stop her with a glance, but it was no good. Finn stepped up and opened the door.

Amanda.

His mother lost the battle to keep a smile off her face. Heading back into the kitchen, she called out, "I'll get cookies."

"Hey, Finn," Amanda said, stepping inside. "I'm Amanda," she introduced herself to Jez.

"Jez."

"Yeah, I know." Amanda gave Jez that same penetrating look she'd given her earlier at the sports complex. Jez just looked back at her and smiled.

"What kind do you like?" Finn's mother asked from the kitchen doorway.

The two girls followed Mrs. Whitman.

"What kind do you have?" Jez asked.

Finn felt outnumbered. He was boiling hot and boiling mad for having his plans interrupted. By the time he reached the kitchen all three of them were jabbering away about how quickly cookies went stale in the

Florida weather . . . something about Girl Scouts . . . Jez mentioned the car wash.

The clock read 8:15.

"I'm beat!" Finn announced from the hall. The two girls glanced over, the conversation interrupted. His mother gave him an *Oh, no you don't!* face.

He said, "I mean, I don't feel so hot . . . Actually, I *do* feel—hot. Like a fever or something."

"But you said you felt fine," Jez corrected him.

He swiped his damp forehead with the sleeve of the bathrobe. "Hot," he repeated. "Did you need something, Amanda?" he asked.

"No. I was just in the neighborhood. Thought I'd stop by."

In the neighborhood? Finn didn't think so. She lived several blocks away.

Jez asked, "Will I see you at the car wash?"

Amanda said earnestly, "Absolutely!" as if Jez had intended this for her.

"Night, then!" Finn said softly, backing up the stairs. "See you both tomorrow, I guess."

Amanda scrunched her face and snarled secretly at him. She did not want to be abandoned.

His mother said, "Finn, we're going to have some cookies—"

Amanda saw his panicked expression; then she

looked at the clock. She understood. "It's okay, we can do it another time," she said. She pulled Jez toward the hallway.

The girls said good-bye. Finn tried to thank Amanda with his eyes.

After the door shut, his mother asked, "Is it true you're not feeling well?"

"Must be why I'm so tired," Finn said.

"Well, get to bed and we'll see how you feel in the morning."

Music to his ears.

The Cinderella Castle shone in the night sky. For all the make-believe in this place, everything seemed so real that Finn briefly understood how the lines had blurred. Even at this hour music floated on the air, coming from Frontierland. Must be a private party, Finn thought. Hadn't Wayne said that private parties had been canceled because of the problems the park had been having? Had Finn imagined that?

A damp evening chill stung the air. It felt like rain was coming. Finn didn't know how his DHI would react to rain. He didn't know a lot of things. Like where to find the others. They had crossed over ahead of him, no doubt, but were now nowhere to be seen. He considered checking the apartment first, followed by the teepee, but then remembered that Philby had mentioned It's a Small World when they had all met at the sports park. They were looking for attractions that corresponded to the sun clue in The Stonecutter's Quill, and though the Sunshine Tree Terrace, the Swiss Family Tree House, and the Carpets of Aladdin were all plausible candidates, Philby and Willa had picked It's a Small World.

The ride had *two* references to the sun. One, in its theme song:

> *There is just one moon*
> *And one golden sun*

Two: the ride's Central American section included a blazing Mayan sun, the biggest sun in the Magic Kingdom.

So Finn headed to It's a Small World first, knowing he would have led the others there had Philby or Maybeck not arrived on time. He found the four waiting outside the attraction, Philby anxiously looking at his wristwatch. Willa waved excitedly as she saw Finn approaching. He heard her say, "I told you he'd make it."

"Sorry I'm late. Trouble at home," Finn said.

As they stepped inside, the ride seemed to wake up. The familiar song started playing, a tune that they all knew by heart.

"It's after closing, so why did the music suddenly start?" he asked.

Philby answered, "Don't worry about it."

Maybeck warned the others that it could be a trap. "Stuff like this doesn't just *happen*."

Finn told them about the music he'd heard coming from Frontierland. "Maybe there's a party over there."

Charlene said, "Wayne told me the rides and attractions are left on at night. Let's just get it over with."

"But the lights are off," Finn said.

Indeed, the farther they moved down the ramp, the darker it grew. Only some emergency floodlights and exit signs were glowing. They provided enough light to see by, but just barely.

They all climbed into a boat, Finn sitting with Philby, Maybeck between Charlene and Willa on the bench behind.

"That song drives me nuts," Charlene said. "The way it gets stuck in my head."

"That song is why we're here," Philby reminded her. "It repeats the word *sun* over and over, and this is one of the original rides."

The boat started moving. As it rounded a bend into the first scene, the music grew louder. Finn and his friends faced hundreds of dolls, all representing the different countries and continents of the world. They were Audio-Animatronics, so their limbs and mouths moved as they sang. The low light cast eerie shadows. An open arch up ahead led into the next scene.

"Do we even know what we're looking for?" Charlene whined.

"A Fastpass back to our normal lives," Maybeck snorted.

Charlene said, "It's creepy in here. *Real* creepy."

Willa pointed. "Hey! Did that doll move?" she asked.

Maybeck said, "They're *all* moving, girl. They're singing."

"No, I mean—*moving*. As in *walking*."

Maybeck laughed. The others followed—even Willa, who was glad for the chance to release the tension they were all feeling.

Their boat passed under the arch and into the next scene.

Behind them, when the DHIs were no longer looking, one of the British dolls leaned forward and snapped its glued feet off the deck of the display. It took a long stride forward. Four others did the same—two from France, two from Switzerland—their mouths moving along with the song lyrics as their feet broke free.

Looking for clues, Willa and Philby called out the various European countries represented by the dolls.

"It's cold tonight," Charlene complained. She crossed her arms.

Finn felt the unusual chill as well. He'd come to recognize that chill. He looked around for any sign of Maleficent.

Philby said, "Think in terms of the fable. It's

originally an ancient Chinese story, so we should focus on Asia, the ride's next scene."

"There!" Willa said, pointing. "I just saw a German move!"

Now Finn looked back as well. "Philby?" he said.

The others turned to look. The boat rocked as they moved.

Charlene screamed. Maybeck said a word he wasn't supposed to say. Philby plunged his hand into the dark water and shouted, "Paddle!"

Behind them, several dozen dolls had broken loose from the scene and were marching toward the water. Toward the boat.

The kids paddled, but the boat didn't move any faster. It was locked onto a track and moved mechanically.

Behind them, the loose dolls banged into each other and tumbled over, but then stood up again. More and more of them leaned and wiggled and stretched and broke free from the various platforms. They marched down through the panoramas, throwing their legs forward like little soldiers, and fell over face-first into the water like lemmings.

The boat dragged slowly forward. The kids could not steer it right or left, nor move it any faster. More wide-eyed dolls fell off the platforms and plunged into the shining water. Miraculously, their arms began to stroke freestyle, and their feet to flutter kick. They were *swimming*.

"They're coming right at us!" Willa shouted.

Finn heard little thuds as the first dolls arrived and banged into the hull of the boat.

"This isn't happening," Maybeck said, trying to sound calm.

"Shut—up!" said Charlene. "Do something!"

There were more of the dolls now—maybe fifty or more, all swimming toward the boat, their national costumes reduced to wet rags. They converged on the boat, stacking one atop the next, higher and higher in a floating pile. One doll flopped over the rail and into the boat. Then another, and another.

The boat passed into the Asia scene. None of the kids was looking for clues now.

The dolls' little singing mouths opened and shut, snapping viciously. A few more tumbled over and into the boat. They were climbing! As they landed, they rolled, crawled, and then pulled themselves up to standing.

One bit down onto Finn's arm, locking its jaw. It drew blood. Finn knocked it off and back into the water.

Two other dolls attacked Philby. Maybeck pushed

them off as if they were live lobsters, then picked one up and threw it. It struck the wall and smashed into pieces.

The other kids cheered.

Charlene and Willa knocked the dolls off the edge of the boat before they could clmb in. Finn tore a biting doll off Philby's leg.

Maybe a hundred dolls were now swimming toward them. They were definitely losing the battle.

Finn glanced ahead through the next arch to the Americas scene. There he saw dozens of dolls, lined up and waiting for the boat.

Maybeck shouted, "We're losing the war, in case anyone's keeping track!" His leg was bleeding from a bite. Willa smacked a doll back into the water. It rose to the surface, turned, and swam again for the boat.

Legions of dolls closed in from all sides.

That chorus of singing screamed in Finn's ears: "*It's a small world after all. It's a small world after all. . . .*"

Finn felt like he was being driven half-crazy by the sound.

"There's a way out of this! We're missing something," he cried. "Think! Everyone *think!*"

"An automatic weapon?" Maybeck suggested.

"A baseball bat," Willa said, grabbing several more dolls and tossing them over the side.

"Form a circle!" Finn ordered. "Back to back!"

Without argument the kids turned back to back, like the five points of a star.

"We must have whatever it is we need to beat them," Finn said.

"Why?" asked the cynical Maybeck.

"Because good conquers evil," Charlene announced. "This is the Magic Kingdom! Finn's right."

"We're missing something," Finn said.

"An outboard motor?" Maybeck quipped. "A stick of dynamite?"

Finn looked up. They were into the Americas scene now, and there on the wall was the huge Mayan sun.

Finn caught himself humming along with the theme song.

Willa heard Finn humming. She joined in with the lyrics.

The dolls kept advancing. Every kid bore a bruise or an open wound. They swept the dolls off the edge of the boat, but it was clearly a losing battle. Dolls jumped for the boat and held on to its sides.

Maybeck banged their little hands with his fists.

Charlene joined in singing:

"There is just one moon and one golden sun—"

Sun! Finn thought. What were they missing?

"And a smile means friendship to ev'ryone—"

Smile! The sun had brought them here. The sun is often shown with a smile on its face. Friendship, Finn thought.

"It's all about friendship!" Finn declared. "The lyrics! Our ability to spread friendship like the rays of the sun!"

"You're out of your mind!" Maybeck roared, smashing an encroaching doll.

"A smile means friendship to *everyone!*" Willa cried. She considered this a moment while still battling the dolls. "We have to smile at them!"

Finn hollered, "Try it!"

Maybeck complained, "You have *got* to be kidding!"

"*Smile!*" Willa and Finn hollered simultaneously.

And with that, all but Maybeck broke into massive fake smiles. They looked like jack-o-lanterns.

Finn watched as the effect of those smiles registered in the frozen glass eyes of the dolls. The expressions on the small faces changed from blood lust to surprise, then curiosity, and then outright affection.

The effect quickly spread through the faces of other dolls. Some stopped swimming. Others turned around.

"Keep smiling!" Finn said, through clenched teeth, his fake smile never faltering.

As the swimming dolls encountered the smiles, they fell back over the side of the boat, back into the water.

Finn and the others began clearing dolls out of the bottom of the boat. Inside the vast room, the song continued, over and over, over and over. Within a few minutes, the boat was cleared. Dozens of dolls floated, lying still in the water.

It's a Small World was going to be closed for "restoration" for quite some time.

The boat passed the giant sun at the end of the Americas scene.

Finn studied it carefully. He saw nothing that even remotely resembled a clue.

examining the equipment on the tables. They were excited because of the break-in in the evening and the confusion it was having with all of the weapons at Dan's Used Cars shows on the blog, one annoyed over something it never built so itself.

Saturday midmorning found the sky without a cloud. A hot sun burned a yellow hole in the rich blue background, promising thunderstorms by late afternoon. The corner parking lot of Dangerous Dan's Used Cars was marked by little red and yellow plastic flags on a string that ran from light pole to light pole, giving the school car wash the feel of a circus. A four-foot-long mock blimp and a big bunch of colorful balloons hovered fifty feet above the asphalt in an effort to draw attention. That was also the job of the girls at the stoplight, who wore jean shorts over their bathing suits and held a sign proclaiming: GIRL SCOUT CAR WASH—$5.

Dan's older-model Hyundais, Fords, and Buicks had been parked to the side, leaving a large area now covered with hoses, buckets, and lots of white foam, as skinny girls struggled to scrub, polish, and shine the cars that lined up for the five-dollar wash. Most of the time the process included a water fight, or a bucket brigade, the general chaos kept under control enough to be fun for all, even onlookers like Finn.

There was already a rumor going around that It's a Small World had been vandalized the night before and would be closed for months. Police were investigating.

Finn stood away from all the water with his friend Dillard, who had taken the occasion to borrow one of his father's Hawaiian shirts. Finn thought he looked pretty cool.

Finn spotted Jez as she left the collection table, where she'd been taking in the money. She kicked off her pair of shorts to reveal a dark purple one-piece Speedo and jumped into the middle of a water fight. Suds flew. The girls giggled and screamed. They hosed down a Volvo and sponged it clean. Now wet, with her hair slicked back, Jez looked over at Finn. She'd known he was there all along.

Noticing this, Dillard said, "You think she likes you?"

Finn said, "She's a girl. No telling what she thinks."

Dillard asked, "You think girls are smarter than us?"

"In some things."

"Like what?"

"Like school stuff, and friendships, and family stuff."

"So we're better at . . . ?" Dillard asked.

"Computer games. And farting," Finn said, cracking up his friend.

"What's so funny?" said a girl behind them.

It was Amanda, wearing a white T-shirt over a

swimsuit and a pair of jean shorts. Finn said hi and she said hi back to both boys.

Dillard opened his mouth to say hello, but belched instead. He'd never been much around girls. Both boys laughed hard.

Amanda dug into the snug pocket of her jeans and pulled out several bills. She handed Dillard a dollar. "Hey, Dill," she said, calculatingly coy, "would you mind getting me an orange soda?"

"No—no—no . . ." he stuttered. "Happy to."

Dillard asked if Finn wanted anything and Finn passed him a dollar, asking for a cola, and thanking him. Dillard took off.

Amanda said, "The nearest orange soda is at the gas station, across the street. It'll take him a while."

"He's not a servant, you know?" Finn said.

"I wanted to hear about It's a Small World," she said. "That *was* you guys, I assume."

Finn said, "You can't say anything to anyone."

"You guys trashed the place?" She took a step back. "Why?"

"It wasn't anything like that. It was—" He felt boxed in. "Impossible to explain."

"Impossible because you *won't*, you mean."

"Impossible because you wouldn't believe it."

"That's not true. Try me."

Finn met eyes with her, considered if this was the right thing to do, and said, "The dolls came alive and . . . attacked us."

Amanda looked stunned, but she did not make fun of him.

Finn returned his attention to the noisy girls and the car wash.

He pulled up the leg of his shorts and showed her where he'd been bitten. Amanda gasped. "Finn . . ."

"I know," he said. "It's getting serious."

"Getting?" she fired back sarcastically.

"And what's worse, we didn't find any clues to the fable."

"You've got to stop this somehow, Finn. It's too dangerous. It's just stupid to continue."

Finn said, "Wish I could, but I don't think I can."

"When I do things I shouldn't do, my mother says I need a new pair of glasses—that I should be looking differently at the choices I make."

A silent alarm went off in Finn's head. He tuned out everything around him—everything but Amanda—and focused on her. "What did you just say?"

"You can't go getting hurt. That's just stupid."

"About the glasses," Finn said.

"Just some dumb thing my mother says."

"Like a different perspective," he said.

153

"Yeah." Her concern mounted. "What if you just stayed up all night and didn't go to sleep? By the time you did go to sleep the Magic Kingdom would be open. Even if you ended up there, it would be safer!"

"And this for the rest of my life, I suppose?" Finn asked. But his brain was working overtime. *A new pair of glasses.*

"Hey, isn't that guy a host?" Amanda asked.

Finn spotted Maybeck at about the same moment that Jez did. Maybeck went over to her, said something, and the two started laughing.

Jez took Maybeck by the arm and led him over to a lemonade stand. She snatched up two cups and offered him one.

Only then, as he peered over the rim of the paper cup, did Maybeck spot Finn and Amanda. His eyes went wide with recognition, and he gave Finn a half wave. Maybeck took two steps toward Finn, but Jez caught him by the arm again, tipped his cup to make him finish his lemonade, and then said something that caused him to crumple up his cup and throw it at her. Jez did the same back at him. Within seconds it evolved into a water fight, with Maybeck at its center.

For some reason Finn wanted to be at the center of that battle. But his focus shifted past the water fight to the street and a car parked there.

Disguising the direction in which he was looking by pretending to scratch his head, Finn said, "Check out that black four-wheel-drive that just pulled up to the curb."

"Yeah?" Amanda said.

"Look closely. Tell me what you see." Finn turned his back on the car completely now.

"Okay. A woman. A grown-up."

"Her hands. On the wheel."

"White gloves," Amanda supplied. "That's a little weird."

"A little?"

"Yeah. White gloves are a little weird, even for Florida."

"Like totally insane," Finn observed. "It's a zillion degrees out."

"You've got to see this," Amanda told him.

Finn glanced carefully over his shoulder. Goosebumps raced up both arms. The driver rolled the passenger window down. Jez, who'd broken away from the water fight, walked stiffly toward the car and stepped up to the window. The driver leaned over to speak to her, giving Finn a better look. Her face appeared unnaturally pale. She reminded Finn of someone, but he couldn't place her.

"Does she look familiar to you?"

"She looks scared," Amanda said.

Finn had been looking at the driver. Only now did he focus on Jez and see her square posture and unexpressive face.

The driver had dark hair, pulled back sharply.

"I can think of one reason you might wear gloves and a ton of makeup," Finn said dryly.

Amanda was off in her own world, still describing Jez. "She looks so unhappy."

"You think that's her mother?"

"No!" Amanda snapped sharply.

"It's possible," Finn said defensively.

"They don't look too friendly to me," Amanda said. "But you're right about the gloves. What's with that?"

Finn didn't say what he was thinking: You might wear gloves and a lot of makeup if your skin was green.

That same Saturday night, the DHIs met at the Indian Encampment across from Tom Sawyer Island. At eight o'clock the park was still open, so they waited for its closing by hiding invisibly inside the teepee.

Finn said, "We'll make our move during the fireworks finale scheduled for eight-thirty. All eyes will be aimed at the sky."

"Why not just wait until closing?" Charlene asked, never one for unnecessary adventure.

Philby answered, "After what happened at It's a Small World, Disney announced that they're increasing security. That means patrols, probably in pairs, maybe in golf carts. We can't afford to get busted. So we cross the park while there are still guests inside. Seeing a DHI will make sense as long as it isn't past closing."

Finn asked the obvious. "How did those dolls come to life?"

Philby answered with a question. "How do *we* come to life?"

"We were *designed* to cross over, if you believe

Wayne. The dolls most definitely were not designed to march around attacking people."

Maybeck said, "A certain woman with a green face comes to mind. A spell?"

Finn found it odd but cool to be invisible, to be nothing but a voice. He wondered if Maybeck had gotten as good a look at Jez's mom as he and Amanda had.

Philby announced, "We can talk about this later. For now, we'll travel in groups, never all five of us together, in case we should get caught. And no matter what, we never go it alone. Two groups. Finn and me. The three of you."

No one objected.

"Maybeck," Finn said, "did you get them?"

"Yeah," Maybeck answered. "Hang on. I left them by the door."

Maybeck's arm appeared by the teepee's open door. He produced five pairs of plastic glasses. "I got here a little early," he said.

"What's with that?" Philby asked.

Finn explained, "Walt's comment to Wayne. And then something a friend of mine said about perspective."

"I don't get it," Charlene said.

"As I recall, Walt's exact words to Wayne were: 'I have plans for this place that should put things into perspective.'"

Finn explained, "In the late fifties and sixties, 3-D

movies were all the rage. Walt was an illustrator and moviemaker. He would have known all about perspective. These days the 3-D movies are some of the coolest things in the parks. I think Walt mentioned it to Wayne for a reason, and Wayne and the others never picked up on it. Perspective; 3-D. You have to wear special glasses. That's why Maybeck and the girls are returning to It's a Small World tonight."

"What?" Charlene said.

"We missed the clue," Finn explained. "We should have found something. Those dolls did not want us in there—or maybe they wanted our attention on them and not the scenery. What if we weren't looking from the right *perspective*?"

Philby asked, "You think the glasses are the answer?"

"Philby and I are going to take the next clue—clouds—while you guys are at It's a Small World checking out the Mayan sun, this time with glasses."

"Isn't going back there a little risky?" Charlene asked nervously.

Maybeck said, "It's the last place they'll look. Lightning doesn't strike twice, and all that."

A coil of wind swirled outside of the teepee, tossing up dust. It quieted the group. They waited a minute or more to feel a chill or see Maleficent, but there was nothing.

Charlene asked, "What do you suppose happens to us back home in bed if we get busted on this side?"

Silence.

"I think my parents are suspicious," Willa announced.

"Mine are, too," Finn added. "They think I'm sneaking out."

"My mom's all uptight," Charlene confessed.

"Going to bed at eight doesn't help things," Maybeck said. "My aunt thinks I've totally lost it."

Finn asked Philby and Willa what, if anything, they'd learned about clouds, the next clue in the fable.

Philby explained, "There are clouds in so many rides. Pooh. Peter Pan. But the ride with the most clouds, and the biggest clouds, is Splash Mountain. That's where Finn and I will start."

"Start what?" Charlene asked.

"When we're inside the attractions," Philby announced, "we all wear the glasses. We'll 'gain a better perspective.' Let's meet back at the apartment at ten. The button is up there. Use it if you have to."

"Listen up," Finn said, moving invisibly toward the teepee door and eventually into the area where he could be seen. "Majority rules. If you guys need to leave the park, then use the remote."

Maybeck asked, "What if it takes all of us at the

160

same time? What if we're wrong about needing to be close to it?"

"Then we'll find out the hard way," Philby said.

"We should get going," Maybeck said anxiously.

"What's the matter?" Charlene asked Maybeck. "You got a hot date?"

Maybeck smirked. "Not with you I don't."

The four others booed him. Maybeck went right on grinning, unperturbed.

Finn and Philby climbed into Splash Mountain's waterway carefully. The dark water was cold. Finn didn't like the feeling at all. "Are we sure," he whispered to Philby, "that this is worth it?"

"Do we have a choice?"

They slogged their way through the first part of the ride, around some turns, and soon encountered a rubber conveyor incline that proved a tough climb. It grew darker the deeper they went into the ride. Aside from his cold, wet legs, Finn felt a different chill all through his body. He considered mentioning it to Philby, but he didn't want to sound afraid like Charlene.

They climbed through a second tunnel, much longer and darker than the first. It had stairs on either side for maintenance and emergency evacuation. Only the orange night sky, and a slight glow from their holograms, offered any light. Once through this second tunnel, they rested briefly before passing a massive tree on their left. In one scene there was a ladder hanging from a branch, with a laundry line to their right. Here the water current was strong and the going more treacherous.

Philby said softly, "I think we ought to float."

"What?"

"Float," he repeated. Philby lowered himself fully into the water and leaned back. The water current quickly carried him away from Finn.

Reluctantly, Finn did the same, not wanting to be left behind.

Both boys maintained their balance and direction by keeping one hand on the steel rail meant to guide the ride's boats.

"I've taken this ride a zillion times," Philby said, "but this is pretty cool."

Finn didn't love being soaking wet, but he too was enjoying himself.

Then they entered a dark scene, a cavelike space filled with Audio-Animatronic figures. The characters, turned off for the night, all stood frozen in midgesture.

"Kinda creepy," Finn said. He'd had enough. The going was perfectly flat here, the current slow. He grabbed the rail and prepared to climb out.

Philby dove forward, splashing them both, and grabbed hold of Finn.

"You can't do that!" Philby warned him. "If we climb out, we'll trip the alarm."

"What alarm?" Finn challenged.

"They use infrared sensors to detect anyone who tries to get out of a log car during the ride."

"But the ride's shut down."

"But is the infrared shut down?" Philby asked. "I doubt it. Besides, there are thirty-six hidden cameras along the ride. If we climb out, we'll be photographed."

"It's pitch-black!"

"But we're not," he said, indicating his own glow. "We'll be photographed, trust me. And if we're photographed, we're identified and busted," Philby said.

"How do you know any of this stuff?"

"Can you spell *Google*?"

"And you waited until *now* to tell me this?" Finn asked.

"I wasn't going to write you a report," Philby snapped back irritably.

Finn's fear grew more intense the deeper they ventured into this cave. They floated faster now as the route twisted and turned. The waist-deep water in the ride's chute was getting deeper; and the water was flowing faster.

"If I remember right, we're going into a small— drop," Philby announced.

Both boys rushed down the drop. Finn's head went underwater, and he heard something grinding. Something mechanical.

He bobbed to the surface. "Did you hear that?"

"The ride's turned on," Philby declared, his voice unsteady. "That means the log cars are moving."

Finn recalled the marching dolls. He had no desire to try to outrace metal boats shaped to look like logs.

Another drop.

The water tried to swallow them. Both boys remained on their backs, arms extended to stay afloat. At the bottom, Finn looked ahead to see another tunnel approaching.

"I don't like this!" he said.

As they neared the tunnel they saw lights and heard music playing. Voices sang, "You gotta keep moving along."

The robot characters were moving; giant creatures with long noses and big bugged-out eyes rocked and danced. One threw a fishing line at the water.

Finn said, "I'm starting to think getting busted wouldn't be too bad."

"Not yet!" Philby announced. "We've got to hang in there."

The two boys swam and bounced and bumped their way along the water route. They passed fake green hills and low-hanging tree branches, and a six-foot-tall rabbit holding a paintbrush. These things looked devilish to Finn as he saw them looming above him.

"The ride takes a total of eleven minutes to complete," Philby said. "If we're halfway along—and I bet we are—then the first log car shouldn't arrive for another six minutes. By that time, we'll only have a couple minutes to go."

"Why doesn't that sound terribly reassuring?"

Next were mountain backdrops and twelve-foot-high bears. Finn looked away, cold and shivering, and anticipated the arrival of a steel log.

"Clouds!" Philby announced.

Finn saw them in the backdrop. They were painted behind a mountain range. He wormed a hand into his pocket and donned the pair of 3-D glasses, just as Philby did.

Nothing. The clouds looked perfectly normal.

Finn squeezed the glasses back into his pocket with difficulty. "This is crazy," he said. "What are we doing here?"

"The more important question," Philby answered, "is who knows we're in here, and why was the ride turned on?"

"If you're trying to cheer me up, you're not doing such a great job," Finn fired back.

A giant rabbit jumped across the scene, and called out loudly, which caused Finn to splash in self-defense. Okay, Finn thought, now I'm defending myself against mechanical rabbits. What if these robots come alive the same way the dolls did? "Okay," he said. "I would like to get out of here!"

"More clouds!" Philby announced.

Finn fumbled with his glasses again. Wearing them, he took in the clouds and sky. Still nothing.

Presently, there were chipmunk voices singing something at such a high pitch and volume that Finn couldn't understand a word. But he could *feel* the logs approaching. Philby kept glancing over his shoulder. He could feel them too.

A low male voice began narrating the ride. The scene became as dark as the inside of a stomach. The boys bounced off the rails and the chute walls. Bruised and cold, Finn grew increasingly desperate. "Exactly *what* are we doing here?" he asked as his head came up from underwater again.

"My bad, Finn," Philby said. "But keep the glasses on. Okay? And keep an eye out for more clouds."

A large wolf wearing a cowboy hat and holding a rabbit was saying something that was probably funny, though Finn wasn't listening. His ears were tuned to the steady groan of the system—the approach of the log cars.

"Maybe we risk the cameras," Finn suggested.

Philby said, "And have our DHIs removed from the park? I don't think so!"

Finn knew this was right. He felt his courage gathering and was glad to have it back.

They slipped down a dip, traveling ever faster in the dark, churning water. Finn saw light up ahead. He felt a profound sense of gratitude. The end of the ride, in sight at last! But then he remembered where they were in the ride. Next up was—

A really *big* drop. The ride's biggest drop of all. Its biggest thrill. Thrill or kill? Finn wondered. He back-paddled, fighting the current.

"That baby's about four stories, straight down," Philby said. "Forty-five degrees. A million gallons of water driving you like a freight train."

Their bodies slapped forward—closer to the edge—despite their vigorous splashing.

"It'll either crush us," Finn said, "or we'll drown."

Philby didn't disagree.

Finn said more loudly, "I said: it'll either crush us, or we'll drown!"

"Yeah," Philby said. "I think you're right." He rolled onto his stomach and tried to swim away from the drop, but it was no use: the water was too fast.

Finn also rolled over and started swimming. He tried for the edge, happy to climb out, even with the risk of getting busted, but the strong current prevented him from reaching the side. He panicked.

Though the two boys swam frantically, they were actually moving with the current toward the drop.

Philby said between strokes, "If we—could get—into a log—"

Was that possible? Finn wondered. It did seem the perfect solution.

How much longer until a log arrived? Finn wondered. He twisted his watch while flapping his other arm in an awkward crawl. Any moment, he decided. Between gulps of disgusting water he said, "Sounds like a plan. Keep swimming!" They were both still slipping backward despite their efforts. The ride's dramatic plummet drew near.

It felt to Finn as if he were being sucked down a giant drain.

"We're not thinking right!" he said. The first log appeared. It looked big and powerful, and it was coming right for them.

Still thinking out loud, Finn said, "We're made of *light*, Philby. Holograms! We're half light. We aren't solid. Wayne talked about Einstein. About how we're more space than atoms." He couldn't see Philby through all the splashing.

A voice surfaced. "I don't think this is the best time to discuss physics," Philby said. "Besides—I probably know more about it than you do."

They heard a loud *bump!* and *whack!* from the dark as the log grew closer.

"If we're mostly light," Finn proposed, "then water current can't affect us. Light moves *through* water; it doesn't get carried off by it."

Driven by his newfound confidence, Finn rolled onto his back and stroked more gently. Slowly, he pulled away from Philby, and with half the effort.

It's all what I'm thinking, he realized.

Philby watched as Finn's glowing body—brighter now—swam past him upstream. In doing so, Philby allowed himself to relax for a moment.

A moment too long.

Philby was sucked down the throat of the final plummet.

Time slowed. Philby tumbled through space and water, holding his breath and then sucking for air. His lungs burned. He couldn't tell what was up or down. Then, amid the swirl of black, a hand appeared. A human hand. Glowing, as if it had been plugged into the wall. Behind that hand another shape formed. That shape was an arm, Finn's arm.

Finn was inside the log car leaning over. The two boys locked hands, and Finn dragged Philby up and into the log. The log threw out a tremendous splash as it reached the bottom of the chute.

By the time Philby had righted himself, now sitting up, the log had snaked through the chute and entered yet another scene. This was the last scene, the most exotic of the attraction.

Finn and Philby scrambled for their glasses.

"How did you do that?" Philby asked.

"I'm not sure. But I think it was all in my head," Finn replied.

Behind the paddleboat, Finn spotted large pink clouds in a big blue sky. His head swirled with the sounds of voices singing "Zip-a-Dee-Doo-Dah." He slipped on the eyeglasses.

There, behind the Showboat, he saw a bunch of clouds. In the middle of one of the biggest clouds he saw several big letters. They appeared to have been spray-painted:

F M E

When Finn lifted his glasses, the letters disappeared.

"Our first clue!" Finn whispered, looking for the exit.

"Where's Maybeck?" Finn asked. The two girls didn't answer right away. They seemed shocked to see him and Philby so wet and so pale.

"We don't know." Charlene sounded frightened.

"The sun!" Philby said. "Did you try the glasses?"

"*Y*, *I*, and *R*. Three letters! They look painted, added on later." Willa replied excitedly.

"Same with us!" Philby said, "*F*, *M*, and *E*. We're definitely on to something."

Finn interrupted their glee. "Where—is—Maybeck?"

Charlene looked worried. "We got to the ride and he said he had something he had to check out. We told him we had to stick together, but he blew us off."

"And he hasn't come back," Willa said angrily.

"Hasn't come back?" Philby asked, finally realizing they had a serious problem on their hands.

"And this was, like, half an hour ago," Charlene said.

"He kept checking his watch," Willa complained. "He was nervous about something, like he was eager to get back."

"Oh, no." Finn heard himself moan.

"The button!" he and Philby said at once.

If Maybeck had taken the button from the apartment with him to the other side, he could leave them all stranded inside the Magic Kingdom until he returned. No one knew if the button would cross over or stay behind. But they didn't want to wait to find out.

The four took off at a run.

They approached the castle with caution. It seemed a likely location for security guards. At night, light streamed up onto its stone exterior, the towering spires pointing like fingers into the dark sky. Crouched behind some thick bushes, just off the ramp that led up to the castle, the kids waited, listening intently and looking in all directions.

Charlene nudged Philby, who nudged Finn. A pair of pirates—figures from Pirates of the Caribbean, not humans—lurked in shadow just inside the castle's first arch. Waiting. Their mechanical eyes never blinked.

Finn whispered, "I know those two! They were part of the group that attacked me."

"You're right," said Philby. "I was there too, remember?"

"You think they're waiting for us?" Charlene asked.

"No. How could they possibly know—?" Finn cut himself off.

"Maybeck," Willa said. "You don't think—?"

"Maybeck is *not* an Overtaker," Philby declared.

"He could be a spy," Charlene proposed.

"No way!" Finn said sharply. "If they're waiting for us, it means Maybeck's in trouble."

"He's been caught!" Willa said.

A chill passed through Finn. He waited a moment to see if it lingered—in case it meant that the witch was nearby. The feeling passed.

Philby said, "Didn't Wayne say something about—"

"Secret ways into the castle," Finn finished for him. "Yes, he did. And he also said if you took a wrong step in Escher's Keep you ended up in the moat. But he never showed us any secret doors."

"I know where one is," Philby announced.

"What?" Finn said, astonished.

"VMK," Philby explained. "I was in this room and I heard these two guys talking about counting stones. *Castle* stones: I'm positive that was it! I had no idea what they meant. But it could be a secret door, a way inside."

"How many stones, and from where?" Willa asked. "We've got to hurry. Maybeck may need us."

"I don't remember, but the point is, there must be a stone you push to get inside."

"But that's in a computer game!" Charlene protested, sweeping one arm across the scene. "This is real life!"

They all looked at her glowing, transparent arm. "Or sort of," she added.

"The game is *part* of real life," Philby said.

"Follow me," Finn said.

Together the four DHIs crept on their stomachs up to the wall of the castle, where they were now out of sight from the waiting pirates.

"Spread out," Finn said. "Push every stone you can reach."

They formed a long line, wrapping around the side of the castle, their backs to Tomorrowland, where the manicured lawn spilled down toward the moat. Finn pushed against the cool stone blocks. He started at knee height and pushed against every stone he could. Then he moved an arm's length toward Charlene, immediately to his right, and started again.

A few minutes into this process Willa called out, "Got it!"

Finn and the others hurried over.

A door had opened in the wall of the castle.

It was pitch-black inside.

Philby said, "Always trust computer games."

With no one stepping up, Finn took the lead. The chilly corridor smelled damp and old.

Philby entered last. He said, "Wait up! We've got to shut this thing."

Willa turned to help him. She found an iron handle sticking out of the wall. She pushed and couldn't move it, then leaned her weight onto it and it rotated toward the floor. The stone door made a sound like fingernails on a blackboard as it closed.

Finn was still very wet from his ordeal at Splash Mountain; his soaked clothes made him very cold now. He felt his way along the cool rock, tripped when he reached some stairs, and warned the others in a dry whisper to look out. Together they climbed the stairs, at the top of which Finn encountered a dead end. It was a stone wall that didn't budge when he leaned against it.

Charlene found an iron handle, just like the one Willa had found at the other end. The two girls leaned against it, and the wall in front of Finn moved open a crack. He and Philby pushed it farther open. . . .

"The throne!" Finn said, recognizing where this door led.

They stepped into the throne room in the waiting area for Cinderella's Royal Table. There were tapestries and flags on the walls. The throne was attached to the hidden door, so that when the door had opened the throne had moved with it. As a team they pushed the door back, but not before Philby had taken a moment to find the hidden switch, a wooden knob tucked away on the back of the throne itself. When this knob was moved, the door tripped open. They tried it once the door was back in place, and sure enough, it came open for them, offering them a way out, if needed.

Minutes later the three others followed Finn up Escher's Keep. He had carefully memorized the way, but took his time, knowing one false step could—

"Thar they be!" came a gruff voice from behind and down below.

Finn and the others turned to see the same two Audio-Animatronic pirates standing at the base of Escher's Keep. They appeared to be overwhelmed by the complications of the stairways, ladders, and platforms, all of which were interconnected in improbable ways.

One pirate was dressed in a blue coat, the other red. The one in red pulled out his knife and pointed up the stairs.

"Hurry!" Charlene cried out.

The sound of clunky mechanical legs echoed up the first stairway.

"We can't hurry," Finn replied. "We make a mistake and we end up in the moat, and that would mean security guards."

The pirates continued to climb.

Philby said, "Besides, they won't figure it out."

But to his amazement, the two pirates made a lucky

guess at the first platform and found the correct stair-way. At the top, the red pirate turned left, but the blue one grabbed him by the shoulder and stopped him. They were frighteningly close to the kids now, only one stairway behind.

Finn remembered how to get onto the upside-down mirror stairs. He stepped on the correct tiles and then tested the stairway with his right foot. It was solid. He climbed, and the others followed. As they came out the end of a short tunnel their images appeared upside down to the pirates below.

"Avast!" the red pirate called out sharply.

He and the blue pirate hurried up the set of stairs in front of them. Charlene charged past Finn, clearly afraid. But Philby, Willa, and Finn watched from their inverted positions as the two pirates reached the next landing and tried to decide on a course. They argued between themselves.

"You wouldn't know east if the sun was rising!"

"No? When was the last time you knew fore from aft?"

They stepped up onto a set of stairs, seemingly proud of their choice, and promptly vanished from sight amid a roar of rough-sounding words.

A moment later, two splashes.

Finn said, "And that would be the moat."

A few minutes later the five kids rode the night-sky elevator to the apartment together. To their confusion, they found the remote button on the coffee table, exactly where Finn had left it.

"Either he came here and sent himself back," Philby said, "leaving us the remote, or—"

"He never left here in the first place," Finn completed.

"That might explain the pirates," Willa said, still wondering if Maybeck was somehow a spy.

"Or it might tell us he's been caught," Philby suggested.

"What about the teepee?" Charlene asked. "Didn't we say if we didn't meet here, we'd meet there?"

"Yes, we did. You're right," Finn said.

"I don't love the idea of going back the way we came," Philby said. "Those clowns could return."

Finn moved over to the silver Mickey plate on the wall by the window. "Wayne used the express lane," he reminded.

"I'm not going first on that thing!" Charlene declared.

Finn said, "Then I will." He hit the plate.

The floor fell out from under him, and he slid in his damp clothes down a twisting, steep exit tube. It was the best tube he'd ever ridden, including every water park he'd ever been to. It leveled off near the bottom, slowing him down, and he popped through a pair of doors and landed on a patch of grass in a shadowy nook outside the castle walls. He rolled out of the way and waited. A moment later, Willa came through. Then Charlene, and finally Philby.

Together, they made their way toward Frontierland, and the teepee, staying in shadow and hiding often.

They called for Maybeck inside the teepee. No answer. Then, at Philby's urging, they climbed inside to get out of sight.

Finn said, "We have to find him before we go back."

"But it's late," Charlene protested. "We have to get back. Listen, he's the one who took off. He broke the rules. Why should we be the ones punished?"

Finn asked, "And if it was you left behind?"

"Shh!" Philby said.

The park suddenly seemed unusually quiet. It felt to Finn as if there were a thousand ears trained in their direction.

A rustle came from the bushes just on the other side of the teepee wall.

They heard footsteps. Someone circling the teepee.

I know you're in there, said Maleficent in her dry, raspy voice. But Finn heard her in his head, not through his ears. *Missing something, are we?* She clucked her tongue. *What a shame you didn't listen and obey. I told you to stay away from here. Nasty children. Nasty little children.*

The footfalls continued around the teepee and reached the front door. The teepee's interior grew steadily colder until the kids could see four plumes of their fogged breath emerging clearly from their invisible bodies.

Across from him, Finn heard a brief but sharp clatter of teeth. Charlene's, no doubt.

The four plumes of fog stopped as all four held their breath. A gangly shadow stretched across the open doorway.

Maleficent's voice sounded like slowly cracking glass. "You should have stayed away while you had the chance." The shadow bent. Her oddly beautiful green face appeared in the open doorway.

Charlene screamed, jumped up, and fled the teepee, suddenly visible. She surprised the witch, who reeled back instinctively. Maleficent lunged at Charlene with her skinny arms and bony fingers, but Charlene was much too fast for her. Maleficent got only a piece of the girl's black T-shirt. The shirt stretched, and Charlene was nearly pulled off her feet. But the shirt tore at the last second, leaving a scrap of cloth in Maleficent's green hand.

Willa fled right behind Charlene. The witch missed her entirely.

Finn saw that Maleficent's eyes were eerily bright. She had surprisingly pretty, high cheekbones, with a high forehead, black hair, and a strong chin. She wore a strange headdress, like two twisting horns that rose from the hood of her cape. Her inquisitive face explored the empty teepee.

"Why can't I see you, you poor simple fools? Hmm? Have you got magic of your own? Do you?" Never taking her eyes off the inside of the teepee, she crouched. Her twisted green fingers with red nails couldn't keep still. She scooped up a fist of sandy dirt from just outside the doorway.

Finn kept in shadow, remaining invisible. He moved carefully and quietly toward the door.

"Now, Finn Whitman, you shall deal with me," the witch said, casting an arc of sand inside.

Briefly, a ghostly image of Philby's left side appeared as the sand struck and stuck to him.

A clever witch at that, Finn thought.

Philby brushed off most of the sand, but not all. His ghostly image remained.

Maleficent stepped over the lip and into the teepee, heading right for Philby.

Finn jumped forward and shoved her to the dirt. It felt like he had rammed into a wall of ice.

"Run!" Finn shouted.

Philby jumped over the witch's legs and sprang out of the teepee. He landed in the dirt, rolled, and came to his feet.

Finn also tripped over the lower lip of the teepee's door. He, too, went down face-first into the dirt.

As Finn came to his feet, a crow flew from the teepee. The bird dove for Finn, its talons like dinner forks. Finn blocked the attack with his forearm and was off at a run.

The crow shrieked, rose high, circled once, and dove again, a flutter of feathers.

Finn ran hard and fast, thinking, She will not scare me. *She will not scare me!*

The bird dove again, this time striking the back of Finn's head, its talons scratching his scalp.

Finn headed for the shore. He hit the water in a racer's dive, knowing the crow couldn't follow. But the crow tucked its wings, lowered its head, and dove for the water's black surface. Finn heard a big splash and then silence behind him.

Charlene, Philby, and Willa, already in the water, swam to shore and clambered up onto the bank and quickly out of sight.

Finn realized the bird—the *witch*—had gone into the water but had never come out.

At that very moment, he felt something wrap

around his ankle. Slimy and cold, it dragged him under.

A giant, black eel. It climbed up Finn's body, wrapped around his middle, and squeezed. And squeezed. Finn tore at it with his hands, but it was like trying to grab a giant slithering bar of soap. The more he fought against it, the more it squeezed. He felt the wind being choked out of him. He couldn't breathe. He was losing consciousness.

Finn heard a loud whine, like an . . . engine. The eel's grip slackened just enough to allow Finn to take a breath.

Above him, Finn saw Philby in one of the jungle boats. Philby held the boat's outboard motor tilted just above the water, its spinning propeller aimed at the eel.

As the propeller was just about to cut the eel like a meat grinder, the beast released its hold of Finn and slithered back down under the dark water. Finn pulled himself from the water as Philby ran the boat up on shore.

"We gotta go, right now!" Philby shouted to the girls. "We've got to get back to the apartment and get out of here."

"Maybeck—" Finn said.

"We can't wait!" Philby shouted.

"That's what I've been telling you!" Charlene said.

"I hate leaving him behind," Willa said, worried.

"We all do," Philby said. "But they know we're here. We've got to leave."

Finn hardly heard any of this. He was not thinking of the water, nor the crow, nor the eel. He was, instead, thinking only this one thing, over and over: She knew my name. *She knew my name.*

Amanda stayed in the lead on her bike. Thankfully, she hadn't asked any questions, and he took this as a sign they were becoming really good friends. He told her only that he had to see Jelly and that she was welcome to come along if she wanted. They locked their bikes beneath a sign that read: CRAZY GLAZE.

"You're awfully quiet today," she said.

"Yeah," was all Finn could think to say.

"You want me to keep her busy while you check around back. Is that about it?"

He nodded.

Amanda entered the store, glancing back at Finn with a worried expression.

Finn found two fire escapes out back, made of slatted iron, servicing several doors.

Finn heard Jelly's distinctive voice through an open window. This was followed by Amanda asking after Terry.

"Terry's not feeling well," Jelly said.

"I brought him some homework," Amanda said. It was a white lie, because in fact she and Finn went to a different school than Maybeck; but she needed a reason to see him.

"That's sweet of you, girl. I'll be sure to pass it along."

Amanda said, "Is it the flu?"

"Not exactly the flu," Jelly answered. "You want to leave him homework, that'd be fine. But right now, I've got a lot do."

"Can I help you?" Amanda offered. "Can I fill in for Terry, if he's not feeling well?"

"Well . . . Terry's asleep upstairs. That would be very good of you, Amanda. Thank you for offering. I'm happy to pay you, though I can't pay much."

Finn climbed up the fire escape. The rail was hot to the touch. If caught, Finn wasn't sure what excuse he'd use, but he'd think of something. At the first landing there was a normal-looking door. Finn knocked gently. Nothing. Then he tried the doorknob; it turned, but he didn't dare open it. That was just plain wrong, and he couldn't bring himself to do it.

Then the obvious hit him: that other landing below the adjacent windows. If he could make the jump . . .

Finn climbed over the rail of the landing, hung on, and jumped. His fingers hooked around the railing. He hung on for dear life, pulled himself over, and collapsed below the first window.

He got to his feet and peered in. He saw a television room with some very nice pottery scattered around. The next window, considerably smaller, was covered on the inside by a thick curtain—a bathroom, perhaps.

Finn moved to the third window and peered inside. *Maybeck.*

He was asleep in bed—*with the shade up and the lights on*, Finn noted—rolled over, with his back to Finn. He had on the same shirt he'd been wearing the night before. Next to the bed, on a side table, Finn noticed a thermometer bulb-down in a glass of water, a face cloth folded into a strip three inches wide, and a copy of the Bible.

Finn knocked gently on the glass. Maybeck didn't stir. Finn tried again, a little louder. Maybeck didn't budge. If Finn knocked any harder, he thought he'd break the glass. Instead, he tested the window. It opened a crack. Again, he faced going inside uninvited. Again, he couldn't bring himself to do it.

But he did slide the window up and stick his head through.

"Maybeck!" he whispered harshly. "Maybeck, wake up!"

"Finn!" It was Amanda's voice, behind and below him. Finn bumped his head on the window frame as he turned to look for her.

"Jelly's coming up there!" Amanda warned frantically. "She *heard* you!"

Finn ducked out the bedroom window. He could hear Jelly coming up the stairs. The footsteps were close now. Finn slid Maybeck's window shut, ducked, and hurried to the railing. He climbed over, paused, and jumped.

For a fraction of a second, it seemed that he'd misjudged the distance, that he would fall, crashing in a pile of broken bones right in front of Amanda. But he made it. He climbed over the railing and hurried down to ground level.

"Finn? Finn Whitman?" Jelly hollered from the upstairs balcony. "What are you doing here?"

"Hello, Jelly!" Finn called back.

"You sneaking around back here?"

"No, ma'am."

"'Cause that's what it looks like."

"I need to talk to Terry," Finn confessed. "It's important."

"You can't. Terry's sick. Not well."

"Sick, or asleep? He won't wake up, will he?"

Amanda snapped her head in Finn's direction.

Jelly said, "You stay right where you are, young man."

Jelly took her time. "Listen," she said, emerging through the back door. "This is not something I want going around school. You understand?" She met eyes with them both. "Terry's got some kind of sleeping sickness."

Finn gasped.

"We can't wake him up. He's not got a fever. Not been bitten by anything. No sweats or shakes." She took a long look up at Maybeck's bedroom window. "Doctor says to let him be one more night. Tomorrow, he goes to the hospital and they start doing tests. But I'm saying my prayers. Nothing seems wrong with him. Doctor says he's fine in all the important ways."

"He's stuck asleep?" Amanda said.

"That's a funny way to put it," Jelly said, "but yes."

Finn wanted to kick Amanda, but she didn't know what she'd said. He had told her nothing about the night before.

Maybeck was still crossed over. Finn struggled to figure out what that meant.

"Can't wake him up?" Finn blurted out.

"That's right," Jelly said.

Finn considered carefully before he spoke. "Listen . . . I don't expect you to believe me or anything, but Terry's condition—it has to do with his being a DHI, a Disney Host, like I am." She studied him thoughtfully but did not interrupt. "I think I can help him. Maybe. Help him wake up."

190

"Is this some kind of joke? Because it's in poor taste, young man. Terry's extremely ill."

"Finn?" Amanda said. "What's going on?"

"Before he went to bed last night—maybe even yesterday afternoon—did Maybeck . . . did Terry . . . get a phone call?"

Jelly took another step away from him. "What's with you, boy?" She was not pleased. She looked on the verge of tears.

"He did, didn't he? And I'll bet he came away from that call excited, didn't he? Because it was from a girl, wasn't it?"

"Her?" Jelly said, pointing at Amanda, not realizing she'd just confirmed that Finn was right.

"No," Finn said softly, "not her." Thoughts crowded his head. "Please don't take him to the hospital until you hear from me tomorrow."

"I'm supposed to trust my Terry to a thirteen-year-old boy?" Jelly said, incredulous.

"Fourteen," Finn said. "I'm fourteen next month."

22

Back riding their bikes, Finn and Amanda pedaled side by side on the sidewalk, slipping into single file whenever they passed a pedestrian. The afternoon slid toward evening, the sun dragging lower in the sky, the first haze of twilight upon them. Finn felt his whole world dimming.

"He's not asleep, is he, Finn?" she asked.

"I don't think so."

"Then what?"

"Trapped over there," Finn said.

"What's that mean?"

"It means we left him, and we shouldn't have, and now he's stuck back there. On this side, he's asleep. Over there, he's still a DHI. Who knows what's happened to him."

"You think he's been caught or something?"

"I hope not," Finn answered. "But this is nothing but bad. Real bad." Finn felt a cool wind on his back. He craned over his shoulder to look.

Though Finn said nothing, Amanda, riding alongside him said, "I feel it, too. Check out your handlebars."

Finn touched his handlebars: *ice cold*. His fingers left small patches of vapor behind as he removed them.

"Just like the car wash," she said.

Finn didn't need to be told what that sudden chill meant.

He scoured the immediate area for any sign of Maleficent.

He saw only cars, storefronts, and power lines.

> *Black cars, red cars, blue cars, and white.*
> *Small cars, big cars, dull cars, and bright.*
> *Where did they come from? Where were they going?*
> *Some cars were driving; some cars were towing.*

"Do you ever think in rhymes?" he asked her, wondering where that had come from.

She glanced over at him, gravely concerned.

"What?" he asked.

"You're thinking in rhymes?"

"So what?"

She answered, "It's one of the signs—it's something. . . ." She caught herself. Her voice trailed off.

"What signs?"

She allowed her bike to fall behind him so far that he couldn't see her. So Finn slowed as well, and they

193

dueled this way: Amanda slowing, then Finn slowing to join her, until they had come to a stop.

"What do you know about this?" he asked, feeling agitated and impatient. "It's a sign of what?"

To their right was a community center and adjoining it an enormous skateboard park with a half pipe, a full pipe, jumps, and four tubs—a landscape of smooth concrete basins, like empty swimming pools, interconnected by ramps and tunnels, where a dozen kids were practicing stunts.

Amanda said meekly, "Rhyming is . . . it's one of the signs of—witches." With that, she rose up onto her pedals and zoomed off, turning in to the skateboard park.

> *The park was full of skaters,*
> *Full of concrete alligators,*
> *Kids in hoards, riding boards.*
> *Sun was sinking, growing later.*

Finn shook his head violently, side to side, trying to clear his thought and push away the rhymes. What had she just said? He couldn't remember. All he could hear were rhymes. One thought found its way through: *Amanda knows something she isn't telling me.* Finn raced to catch her.

This is weird,
Like a man with a beard.
Green skin and pigs' eyes,
Frog legs and fireflies,
A dark cave with loud cries.
A girl with tears in her eyes.

Finn caught up to her. Amanda's eyes were red. She'd either been crying or affected by the speed of her riding.

"Amanda . . ."

"I can't tell you," she said.

A motorized minibike zoomed noisily around the corner and dropped into the skate park. The rider was thin and wore a black leather top and pants and a black helmet with a silver-mirrored visor that hid his face.

The minibike came straight at them, showing no signs of slowing. On the contrary, it was on a collision course.

Amanda rose up onto her pedals and dropped her bike into the first big concrete bathtub. Finn followed. They climbed the opposing wall and flew up, airborne.

The minibike followed.

Finn rose from his seat, balanced the bike in the air, tipped forward, and dove into the next big concrete basin.

Amanda dropped into the half pipe to the left.

Separated like this, the minibike driver had to choose; it came at Finn.

The other boarders and bikers stopped what they were doing and watched the contest.

Amanda flew down the steep wall of the half pipe, picking up speed and launching into a high jump. Finn, parallel with her now, yanked his front wheel in midair and changed direction upon landing. He joined her, following inside the full pipe.

As the minibike entered the full pipe, Finn found the screeching whine of its motor deafening.

Out the end of the pipe, riding together now, Finn and Amanda raced to the bottom of the third tub, pushed down onto their seats by centrifugal force. As they raced up the opposing side, they lifted, tipped their weight in unison, and reversed their bikes. Aimed back down into the deep basin, the minibike whining toward them, Amanda bravely reached over with her left arm and grabbed Finn by the forearm. Finn returned the grip.

"You ready for this?" she asked.

"On three," Finn said.

They released their brakes on the count of three, zooming toward the oncoming minibike, their arms extended and ready to clothesline the rider.

The bikes flew down. The minibike wound its way

toward them. Amanda and Finn screamed in unison. At the last possible second, the rider dumped the minibike in a flurry of sparks, slipping under their clasped arms and between the two bikes.

The few onlookers let out a wild cheer.

Amanda and Finn stopped at the top of the basin and looked back.

The driver, lying next to the minibike, appeared okay. He (she? it?) stood up, brushed off, and gestured toward the two. Finn felt a pulse of cold fill him. A *familiar* cold.

Amanda shouted something that sounded like a foreign language. She crossed her arms and then threw them forward toward the rider, and the cold stopped abruptly. The leather-clad rider was lifted from the ground and thrown to the concrete.

"Ride!" Amanda hollered at Finn. "Ride, and don't look back!"

Finn pedaled off, wondering if he'd just seen Amanda do that.

"Who *are* you?" he shouted, as their bikes reached the street.

"We've got to split up," she said. With that, she pedaled furiously away from him.

A t dinner that night, Finn brooded at the table, unable to take his mind off recent events: Maybeck's sleeping sickness, Amanda's mysteries, the letters they'd found secretly hidden at both It's a Small World and Splash Mountain.

Watching him, his mother wore a look of curiosity, while his father, in typical fashion, ate quietly. Finn stabbed at his food and moved it around on his plate, hoping it might appear eaten.

"How was school today?" his mother asked. Every night, the same question. Next would come: did you do anything fun today? What are your friends up to?

"Did you do anything fun today?" she asked brightly. She couldn't stand it when Finn was quiet like this.

"I don't know," Finn answered honestly. "It's all right, I suppose."

"You can do better than that," his father said. His father always thought Finn could do better at everything. He seemed always to be riding Finn about his grades or his performance on the soccer field. He talked about college scholarships like they were some kind of religion.

"I'm good," Finn said, pushing back his plate. "May I be excused?" Another part of the secret code. He had no chance of leaving the table without these passwords.

"No snacks later, sweetheart. This is dinner."

"I know," Finn said. He stood up from the table and grabbed his plate. Suddenly his head went all rubbery, as if all his blood was draining from him at once.

He thought he might pass out.

"Finn?" His mother's voice, but in the next county.

Then there was her painted mouth moving above him, her voice sounding detached and several octaves lower than normal, like a tape playing at half speed. She'd rushed to his side.

The lights in the room dimmed. A power failure? He saw his father, chewed food in his open mouth, looking . . . scared.

"Finn, dear?" his mother said.

"I'm . . . fine," he replied.

His mother hovered over him. He felt his parents taking him under his arms and leading him upstairs. Finn's feet flapped and dragged. He felt useless.

They led him toward his bed.

"No! No! I don't want to go to sleep!" But his eyes felt *so heavy.* . . .

He closed his eyes, and it happened again.

Finn awoke on the same park bench where he'd first met Wayne, at the end of Main Street, across from the fire station. It was nighttime, though the park remained open.

He looked down to see his arms and legs faintly glowing: he was his DHI self. Some kids saw him, and he knew he was in for trouble if he didn't get out of there.

A flash of light to his right. Finn strained to see through the thick crowds—always so many people!—and . . .

Yes, there it was again: another flash of light. For an instant, the crowd parted and he saw Philby waving.

Finn dragged himself heavily across the street, still feeling sluggish, leaving the curious kids behind, and caught up with Philby.

"I thought that was you," Philby said, pocketing a flashlight.

"You don't look so hot," Finn said.

"Have you tried a mirror?"

"Another brownout?" Finn asked.

"I assume so."

"We're early," Finn said.

"Yeah, but if we're here, chances are, the girls are too. We should check the apartment and the teepee."

"But let's do it together," Finn suggested.

"Maybeck?" Philby asked.

"I went to his house," Finn answered. "He's asleep in bed and they can't wake him up. Tomorrow morning they're going to take him to the hospital and start running tests. We've got to find him before that. Who knows what they'd do to him?"

"Maybeck was caught," Philby said. "And it wasn't security. It was the Overtakers. It has to be. Wayne said Maybeck's our computer guy. We know he's been poking around. The Overtakers don't want him messing with the DHI server. The brownouts—our feeling lousy like this. That's the server doing that. The Overtakers are trying to—"

"Kill us?" Finn said.

"Slow us down. Scare us away." He didn't sound convinced.

"Then I'd say it's working," Finn said.

"So where do we start? The apartment or the teepee?"

Finn looked past Philby at the glowing windows above the fire station. "Neither," Finn said. "Follow me."

* * *

Finn climbed the stairs on the side of the firehouse two at a time.

"I should have thought of this before. He told me he lived here."

"Who?"

Finn knocked on the door.

Wayne answered.

Philby and Finn were welcomed inside. It was a cozy room, all wood and brass, that felt like something from a ship.

Wayne wore a heavy wool sweater, khaki pants, and Mickey-and-Minnie slippers. There were books everywhere, and no television or even a radio. The bed was up in a loft in the very peak of the roof.

"Wow!" Philby said, looking around. There were Disney toys scattered around, antiques that went back decades. A fabric wall hanging showed off over a thousand Disney pins.

"I wondered how long it would take you to look me up," Wayne said. It seemed almost as if he'd been expecting them. There were three teacups by the stove and three chairs set out facing one another.

Wayne poured them some tea and gestured for the two boys to sit down.

"Can you help us find Maybeck?" Finn asked.

"Was it Maleficent?" Philby asked.

Wayne's eyebrows arched. He did not answer Philby directly. "What do you know about her?" He had owl-like circles beneath his ice-blue eyes. He looked ominous and menacing now instead of like the silly old guy Finn had first thought him to be. He smiled thinly and said, "Amazing things happen when we put our minds to it. There is a saying that seeing is believing. But believing is seeing, as well. And touching. And hearing. Connecting."

"The witch, Maleficent, has something to do with this," Finn said. He told Wayne everything that had happened recently.

"Apparently she has *everything* to do with this," Wayne agreed.

"The Overtakers," Finn tested. "There are other Overtakers besides Maleficent."

"Too many to count."

"Like the pirates."

"Worker bees, is all. The pirates don't matter much. But you must underestimate nothing, no one. Conviction is the better part of intent. Few battles are won by strength alone. Cunning and knowing your resources can help you overpower the most powerful."

"How do we stop Maleficent?" Philby asked anxiously. He sipped the tea, liked it, and drank some more.

"Don't get ahead of yourselves," Wayne said.

"Maybeck," Finn said.

"They won't want anyone to see him. Nor to hear him, should he call out," Philby continued.

"Someplace dark and noisy," Finn said.

"One of the attractions!" Philby said. "Like Pirates of the Caribbean! The pirates took him!"

"It's not dark enough," Finn said. "And where would they hide him?"

"On the boat, maybe," Philby said.

"Possibly," Wayne said, though his tone of voice suggested that he didn't give the idea much credence.

"Well, listen, Obi-Wan," Philby said sarcastically. "Why don't you tell me and Luke here where to find him, and we'll make for hyperspace."

"Warmer," Wayne said to Philby, though he engaged Finn with his eyes.

"Space Mountain," Finn said. "Pitch-black and superloud."

Philby sat forward excitedly. "Is he right? Is that where they've got him? Brilliant!"

Wayne sipped his tea, looking over the cup. "I have no idea where your friend is being kept. It's a big park. Very big."

Finn thought for a moment and then said, "More important, it might be like the teepee inside there. A

DHI shadow. That would make Maybeck invisible—easy to hide, to say the least."

If Wayne knew any answers, his face revealed nothing.

"It's a place to start," Finn said. "We have to start somewhere."

Wayne said, "They're keeping you from solving the fable. You see that, don't you? Distracting you."

"And if we solve it?" Philby asked.

"*When* we solve it," Finn said, looking right at Wayne.

"Rescue your friend. Solve the fable. Only then will we know what's expected of you."

Finn and Philby wouldn't be entering Space Mountain through the front door. Wayne told them of a trap door that existed in the very top of the pointed dome roof. The roof hatch was used by Maintenance, and to his knowledge had never been locked.

If the boys could climb to the first level of the dome—about fifteen feet up—they'd reach a metal ladder that ran up the back of the dome to the pinnacle. From there, they could enter the ride's interior.

At Wayne's suggestion, the boys borrowed some ropes from the firehouse. They then snuck through shadows, carrying the heavy ropes over their

shoulders, and reached the backside of the attraction.

Crouching in some bushes, looking at the steepness
of the roof and the small metal ladder that led to the
top, Finn said, "The Overtakers have got to assume
we'll come for Maybeck."

"But to them we're kids, don't forget."

"They'll have patrols. Cameras, maybe."

"So when we do this, we do it quickly."

The roof was shaped something like a magician's
hat, with a wide brim and a conical peaked crown.
There were antennae on top.

Philby proved his climbing skills by tossing one of
the ropes over a metal railing on the brim part of the roof.
He tied it off. "We're set," he announced, waving Finn
over.

Finn, who was not big on heights, shinnied up the
rope. In short order he reached the brim of the roof. He
threw a leg over and pulled himself up.

Philby followed silently and without incident.

They kept away from the edge of the roof, where
they might be spotted, as Philby pulled up the rope and
stashed it out of sight. Quickly they ascended the white
metal ladder that ran to the peak. Attached to the roof,
it ran at the same steep angle as the cone.

They reached the top, and sure enough, there was

a metal trap door, exactly as Wayne had described it.

Finn reached for the handle and pulled. It lifted open. He peered down into a black square, completely void of light.

"Who's going first?" Philby asked, his voice breaking.

Finn led the way down the metal ladder. Philby followed and they descended silently. After a moment, Finn's eyesight began to adjust. They were way up inside the pointy-hat part of the domed ceiling, a gigantic space that contained the entire Space Mountain roller coaster track. He made out a few red exit signs, but they were not bright enough to see by.

The track was a tangle of metal fringed by catwalks and supported by towering I-beams and steel columns. Finn felt as if he were inside a complicated clock. They reached a catwalk—a path that led along the roller coaster track, with a metal mesh floor—and followed it to a set of metal stairs leading down. This connected to another catwalk. Suddenly it felt as if they'd entered a maze.

"This is crazy," Philby whispered. "The place is *huge*. Maybeck could be anywhere."

"I'm not so sure about that," Finn said. "Agreed, it's huge, but look around. Where are you going to hide him?" Now that his eyes had fully adjusted, he could make out the size and scope of the complicated track.

But it was all exposed and open—not a good place to hide someone.

"Hey!" Finn said, holding out his hand. *Seeing* his hand.

"Yeah," Philby said, "I know." But he moved his own arm around to show Finn that the metal broke up the imaging. His arm appeared to be in pieces, separated by black stripes. The DHI projection in here was spotty at best.

"You take that side," he instructed Philby. "We'll meet in the middle over there." He pointed out a low spot in the ride where the track turned sharply left.

"If something goes wrong," Philby cautioned, "we get out of here and meet at the apartment."

"Got it."

Finn descended yet another ladder and then followed a catwalk toward one of the exit signs, using it as a beacon. The catwalks reminded him of submarine movies.

If he were hiding someone, Finn thought, he'd stash his hostage close to where guests made the most noise—in a place where any shouts for help would likely go unheard. Finn searched the track overhead for just such a spot. Then he leaned over the rail of the catwalk and looked below. Not far below him, and slightly to his left, he noticed an indistinct dark shape that, as he approached, he realized was geometric: a large rectangle. Now he recognized it as a booth or storage room. Like the catwalks, its walls were of heavy wire mesh. Finn climbed over the rail, lowered himself and dropped to a catwalk below. He reached out and touched the wire mesh—it was covered in a greasy dust that stuck to his fingers. It looked like a large garden shed, about six feet tall, ten feet deep, and fifteen feet long.

On the front of the shed a heavy canvas was hung that prevented Finn from seeing inside. The canvas was tied down on the inside. Finn located the only door, which was wood-framed and also covered with wire mesh. He felt his way down the door and struck a piece of heavy metal: a padlock.

Locked out.

"Pssst!" Finn tried to signal Philby but got no answer. Finn looked around, off into the dark, realizing he'd completely lost track of his friend. He tried again. "Pssst!"

A muffled voice made him spin around: it was coming from *inside* the screened shed.

"Philby!" Finn tried again, a little louder. He heard the scuffle of feet.

"Mmms . . . hmmm . . . heggg . . . warfff," said the muffled voice behind him.

"Maybeck? It's me, Finn!" Finn struggled with the lock again, and then remembered: he didn't need to unlock the door.

Finn closed his eyes and concentrated on his being made of light, nothing but light, and he walked through the wall, just as he'd swum through the water without feeling the effect of the current.

Once through, he realized how much darker it was inside the shed because of the canvas. Finn felt his way around, stepping over boxes and coils and pieces of metal.

The muffled calls for help became more urgent.

"I'm right here," Finn said, turning toward the sound.

Close by now, Finn squatted, felt around, and touched an arm.

He jumped back, fell over and knocked something loose, making a loud sound.

"Nnnnnnnn," said Maybeck. Wiggling as he was, a piece of Maybeck's DHI, his left side, suddenly showed. Finn lunged forward and untied the gag.

"Oh, man," Maybeck said, the gag slipping off.

"You okay?"

"No, I'm famished! And I'm thirsty. But thank you, man, thank you!"

Finn untied Maybeck's wrists and ankles.

Maybeck said, "Let's book it."

"We gotta find Philby. He's in here someplace, looking for you too."

Maybeck pulled on the locked door, but it didn't budge. "But how'd you . . . ?"

"Right through the wall," Finn explained.

"That's fine for you, but what about me? I can't go through a dumb wall."

"Sure you can."

"No, I can't."

"You're going to have to."

Maybeck stared at the dark canvas and the locked door. "Are you telling me I could have just walked out of here all along?"

"Not if you'd convinced yourself you were trapped," Finn replied.

Maybeck reached out. His hand struck the canvas.

"You've got to lose the attitude, Maybeck," Finn instructed. "You're only hitting that wall because you think that's what's supposed to happen."

"I don't have an attitude." He waited for some support from Finn. "Do I?"

Finn demonstrated. First, he reached out and touched the canvas; then, he reached over a second time, and his hand and forearm passed right through up to his elbow.

"I do not have an attitude," Maybeck repeated.

"Prove it," Finn said. He was worried about the noise Philby was making trying to get over to the shed. The bumps and bangs seemed amplified in this echo chamber.

On Maybeck's sixth try, he walked through the wall of the enclosure. Once on the other side, he bent over, as if in pain.

"You okay?" Finn asked.

Giddy with the accomplishment, Maybeck started giggling. "What a dumb jerk! I could have walked out of there all along."

"Not with your hands tied. That rope is from this side. The rope would have stopped you from getting through the wall."

Maybeck blurted out. "It was Jez."

"What was Jez?"

"She called," Maybeck said.

"Called your house," Finn said, having figured out some of this on his own. "Last night, just before you crossed over."

"Said she'd meet me."

"When you checked your watch . . ." Finn said, speculating. "The line you fed us about having a hot date . . . You really *did* have a hot date."

"I ditched the girls at It's a Small World. We were going to meet—Jez and me—at the carousel. But all of a sudden I was so *cold*. I could barely move—like slow motion."

"Yeah, cold," Finn said. He was thinking: been there, done that.

For nearly a week, the kids met inside the park after going to bed, but only for a matter of minutes. As quickly as possible they would use the button to return home, having looked for no more clues. They caught up on sleep. They did their homework. They rejoined their families. Maybeck's abduction had worn them out and frightened them to the point of not wanting to continue. They overcame their reluctance only when Philby showed up at one of their meetings telling of a newspaper story he'd read about an electrical company power station that had been "attacked" and drained of all its power.

"It's not a coincidence," he told the others. "This is spreading beyond the park."

On Saturday morning, the girls decided to use their complimentary passes to enter the Magic Kingdom legally. As kids, not DHIs. That felt safer. They wore disguises in order to keep fans from spotting them and carried 3-D glasses to wear on the rides.

As they stood outside, waiting to board The Many Adventures of Winnie the Pooh, a cartoony voice came over the speakers saying, "Happy *winds* day." It was this, and other references on the ride, that had led them to pick it as the most wind-oriented ride in the park. Wind was the third clue in the Stonecutter's fable.

They sat down in the car, and the ride began. Black lights made their teeth glow white and their skin and clothing almost disappear.

"Glasses," Willa announced, donning hers. Charlene followed. "You look right. I'll look left," Willa coached. "If we see any letters—big letters in an unexpected place—we're supposed to write them down."

Charlene said, "I've got it." She sounded nervous, and Willa understood her concern. The rides had been anything but friendly since this hunt had begun.

As they traveled along, doors swung open to admit their car into each new scene. Reaching the third scene, Charlene realized she heard no one talking. She looked back and saw there was no one in the car behind them. Rising to her knees, she saw no one in the car behind that one either.

Yet the line out front had been packed.

"Willa . . . ?"

"Over there!" Willa said, pointing out a large, colorful tree drawn onto a panel. She lifted and dropped her 3-D glasses onto her nose in order to make sure—but yes, there was a single letter drawn into the leaves of the tree.

She called out quickly, "It's an *S*!"

"*S*?" Charlene asked, puzzled. "But look *behind* us!"

Willa was too excited to look back.

"There's no one behind us," Charlene announced. "No one in the cars behind us. Why not?"

Willa pulled a folded piece of paper from her pocket and scribbled down *S*. As she did, a drop of water appeared on the paper. Then another. And another.

"Behind us!" Charlene cried urgently.

Willa looked back. She looked up.

More water.

The doors to the next scene popped open and shut. They were in the rain scene. Rain drawn in long lines down the walls. Rain falling from the ceiling.

"Since when is this part of the ride?" Willa complained, stuffing the paper into her pocket.

At that moment, their car stopped moving.

"What's happening?" Charlene whined. "Why are we stopping?"

The few light raindrops changed into a downpour. At first it seemed funny. But then it wasn't simply rain, it was a torrent. Buckets. Both girls gasped for breath through a steady stream of water pouring down onto them. It was hard to breathe without coughing.

"This isn't right!" Willa cried.

Now the water beneath their car began to rise. The car lifted, floating. Charlene lunged forward nervously, nearly capsizing them. She leaned out of the car and pushed against the large doors to the next scene.

"They're stuck! They won't open."

As the water rose at an astonishing rate, the car floated higher and higher. Sparks flew as electrical wires were submerged.

"Stay in the car!" Willa hollered. Light sockets sparked and zapped. "We could be electrocuted!"

The car floated quickly toward the ceiling. Willa understood the worst of it: the higher they rose, the less available the air would be. They would either drown or suffocate.

"Willa . . ." Charlene moaned.

"I know."

The car rose higher still.

Sparks flew again as more lights went under.

"We're in trouble," Willa said, surprisingly calm.

"Duh!"

"We need a way out."

"Just now occurred to you, did it?"

The rain fell like a waterfall—the car was now less than three feet from the ceiling. Another foot or two and the car would be pinned with the girls inside it.

Why won't the doors to the next scene open? Willa thought.

"Sit still," she warned Charlene.

Studying the large scene doors, Willa stood up in the car. Charlene hollered at her to sit down as the car threatened to tip over.

Willa grabbed the overhead pipes to stabilize the car. She then pulled hand over hand to draw the car closer to the doors. But as the water rose, with so little room, Willa was forced back down into her seat.

No time!

Water streamed down her neck and shoulders as she spotted a sawed-off length of pipe jammed across the top of the large doors, blocking them and holding them shut. The "rain" was nothing more than the emergency sprinkler system gone wild. All this trouble could be easily explained: the sprinklers malfunctioning. Maleficent had done her job well.

Willa pulled on the sawed-off length of pipe but couldn't budge it. She called for a stunned Charlene to help as the water rose steadily higher.

Together they pulled.

Water spilled over the side of the car, quickly filling it.

Willa chanted, "One—two—"

On '*Three!*' both girls heaved on the pipe, pulling it free.

The doors blew open. The girls fell back into the car as a few thousand gallons of water rushed into the next scene, and the car rode the leading edge of the wave like a surfboard.

The plume of water spun and turned and twisted its way out toward the ride's finish, leveling off as it reached the exit. Their car lowered and settled into the track, right where it had started.

The waiting guests stood there drenched head to toe. A lake of water had flooded the pavement outside the attraction.

In all the confusion, the two girls hurried from the car and ran for their lives.

Late that afternoon, nearing the dinner hour, the DHIs met in Finn's guest room in the Virtual Magic Kingdom. This had become something of a routine for them. Lately, Charlene's and Willa's characters took the couch while Finn, Maybeck, and Philby stood and moved around the room.

A text bubble appeared above Willa. She told them about nearly being drowned at Winnie the Pooh, and that she had called Philby prior to this meeting and had told him about the *S* she and Charlene had discovered. It was Philby's job to make sense of the clues.

Philby's character explained that he'd run the letters *F M E Y I R* and *S* through an Internet anagram generator. The program rearranged the letters into every possible combination and then printed up the results.

philitup: there are only two decent possibilities. MY FRIES and YES FIRM. Neither makes much sense.

Finn: So we need more. The last clue mentioned in the fable is "stone." Any ideas what ride that might be?

philitup: I thought about Tom Sawyer Island. There

are rocks over there. But then I realized it has to be Thunder Mountain. I mean, give me a break! Talk about rocks. That place is all rocks.

Finn: So we'll start there, at Thunder Mountain—Philby and I.

Mybest: Sounds good to me.

angelface 13: But we'll all cross over, just as we do every night. Are we supposed to just wait for you?

Finn could just imagine Charlene whining as she typed.

Finn: At some point, we'll need to get Wayne. He lives above the fire station. By the time Philby and I are off Thunder Mountain, we should have all the letters. We'll get back together and try to solve the riddle. If we do, if we're successful, we'll need Wayne. He should be told what's going on.

Mybest: I can get over there and give him a heads-up. The girls can keep a lookout from the apartment. It looks right down Main Street. We'll set up some kind of signal in case they see trouble. That'll help.

philitup: sounds like a plan.

The five characters formed a huddle in the middle of Finn's guest room. They all put their hands into the center, like players on a sports team. And then they left the room.

Finn headed downstairs and found his mother bent over the kitchen sink doing dishes.

She asked, "Do you want to help me?"

"Sure."

Finn bagged and took out the trash. He cleaned the kitty litter. He was about to put some dishes away when his mother reminded him where his hands had just been; so he washed his hands and was putting away some dishes when she said, "We need to talk."

"Sure."

"Let's sit at the table."

The table? This was bad—very bad.

"I need something explained to me, and I want you to be honest," she said. The kitchen table grew impossibly long in his mind, as if his mother were a judge way down at the far end.

"Okay," he said.

"The laundry."

"Yeah? What about it?"

"I'm your mother, Finn. Each day you come home from school, I look at you, both because I love you and because it's my job to keep your clothes clean. If your pants are clean, for instance, I say nothing and you can wear them another time. If they're dirty, I ask you to put them in the laundry."

"So?"

"Remember, I need you to be honest. That's more important to me than anything else."

"Mom . . ."

"I'd rather not involve your father, but if you insist on lying to me, I most certainly will." She paused and then said, "Your clothes are dirtier in the morning than they are when you go to bed. A week ago, they were damp and smelled like . . . well . . . awful."

Evidence! He hadn't thought about this aspect of his adventures. He had tried to keep himself looking the same: taking showers in the morning to get the dirt off. Yet he had just tossed his clothes into the hamper. Now he saw the stupidity of that.

"It's not what you think, Mom."

"Enlighten me."

"I haven't lied to you. Not exactly."

"You either have or haven't. There's no in-between when it comes to the truth."

"I have not snuck out of the house. I promise."

He saw a tremendous relief in her eyes, but still her voice quavered, "Finn . . ."

"I swear. Mom, I have not snuck out of the house. I told you I wouldn't, and I haven't."

"Finn . . ."

"I *have* worn my clothes to bed a few times in the past couple of weeks. If they look more wrinkled in the morning than they did when I went to bed—"

"Wrinkled? They're *filthy*! Wet. With holes in them. I'm sorry, but that doesn't sound like the truth to me. Let's start over, one more time. Please, trust me. You can tell me whatever it is. Whether or not we involve your father . . . well, we'll see."

"It stays between the two of us?" Finn asked nervously. "I gotta hear you say it, Mom."

"It stays between the two of us," she said.

"Okay, but you're not going to like it."

"Finn! Just *tell* me."

Finn drew in a deep breath, wondering if he actually should tell her. What choice was there? The evidence had busted him; he needed to explain it without getting himself into more trouble.

He said, "Something crazy happened when they made the DHIs out of us—the five kids." He watched her face grow curious and concerned. "When we go to sleep, we aren't exactly asleep. We wake up in Disney World . . . as DHIs—as holograms." Now she seemed to be fighting a smile. "Trouble is, whatever happens there, carries over here. So when I get all dirty there, I end up dirty back here. But you can't tell Dad, remember? You promised."

For a moment it didn't appear she was breathing.

Then, her lips unpuckered, her nostrils flared, and she grinned. "That is the lamest, though the most creative excuse you've ever tried."

Finn stared at her, dumbfounded. So this is what he got for telling the truth. "Mom, it's the truth."

She tried to compose herself, lost it to a creeping smile, and then suddenly grew very serious as Finn's expression did not change. Now she seemed to believe him.

"The burn you saw on my arm? A laser fired at me inside the park, at night. I have a bruise on my leg where a doll bit me."

"A doll?" There was that twitching smile again.

"It's a Small World. One of those dolls."

"I see."

He couldn't understand it. She didn't believe him.

"You said you wanted the truth," he reminded her. Maybe she thought he was losing his mind. "No doctors," Finn said, defending himself.

"You actually believe this?"

"How do you explain my muddy clothes? Huh, Mom? I am *not* sneaking out. I knew you wouldn't believe me!"

His reasoning clearly perplexed her.

"Let me get this straight," she said.

He interrupted. "You won't get it straight. Because *we* haven't gotten it straight—the five of us. You can't stop it, Mom. I can't stop it. None of us can. It just happens. And until we solve—There's stuff that's got to happen before this is going to stop."

"Finn, you're worrying me."

"You promised you wouldn't tell Dad."

"But I thought . . . I don't know what I thought."

"You promised. Just remember you promised." He added, "The wet clothes. Tom Sawyer Island. You know that lake around it?"

"This is not funny, Finn. Okay? A-plus for originality. You really had me going. Now, please tell me the truth. The *real* truth."

"'There's no in-between when it comes to the truth,'" he said, quoting her. "If you can't handle the truth, it's not my fault."

"Finn, do not leave. Not like this," she demanded as he stood from the kitchen table. "Where are you going?" she called out, stopping him in the doorway.

Finn turned and faced his troubled mother. "There's only one way to end this, to get this over with." He hesitated, thinking of all the things he could explain if she would only believe him. "I'm going to sleep."

If Finn had to tackle Thunder Mountain with any of

his fellow hosts, he was glad it was Philby. Philby was the kind of smart that made other school kids ask him to do their homework. By now he would have done as much Internet research on the ride as possible. They'd both ridden it dozens of times. But climbing around the ride at night was altogether different, as they'd learned the hard way at It's a Small World and Splash Mountain.

They stood at the entrance to the ride. Moonlight glinted on the tracks. Finn said, "The letters we're missing could be anywhere. On any *stone*, any rock."

"You got it."

They were surrounded by maybe ten thousand rocks.

"Anything I should know before we start?" Finn asked, knowing there had to be.

Philby said, "There are security cameras. A lot of them. Some are infrared and can see at night. And it's like Splash Mountain: we can't leave the track. That's all we've got to worry about."

Finn knew that wasn't the case, but he didn't say anything. He didn't want to jinx them.

The boys started down the roller coaster's track. It rose and twisted and turned, extremely tricky to walk. They both wore their 3-D glasses and looked everywhere possible for clues. Philby, in the lead, occasionally stopped and listened and looked around. It made Finn nervous.

They continued along the empty roller coaster track, sometimes walking almost crablike. They made it through two long climbs without incident. The roller coaster rose higher and higher.

"Where are we?" Finn asked.

"A little over halfway, I'm thinking."

They stopped to rest. The moonlight shone down onto the red rocks. Neither boy saw any letters written on the stone.

Finn said, "Hey, guess what? We haven't got a clue."

"That's a sick joke."

They entered a canyon with steep walls. It grew darker the farther in they went. Finn felt his nerves tighten. He didn't exactly love roller coasters. Walking one in the dark didn't help matters.

The boys lowered themselves down a short drop in the tracks as the canyon widened. The scene was part desert floor, with cactuses and mining equipment, and part rock canyon. Massive stone walls rose on all sides.

"Too cool!" Philby said, lifting and dropping his glasses onto his nose and pointing.

At first, Finn thought he meant the Indian drawings and the dinosaur fossil that stuck out from the farthest rock wall.

But then he looked more closely. The letters: *T*, *P*, *N*. Each letter appeared to be engraved on its own rock in the ride's rockslide.

Finn checked with and without the glasses. This was definitely their clue.

"Way to go! Okay, that's it," he said. "Let's get out of here."

"We're closer to the end than the start of the ride. It's over this next rise. We'll get off the tracks there without being seen by the cameras."

"Okay. Let's just go," Finn said, wanting to be gone. Something wasn't right here. He couldn't identify what it was, but he felt it.

They struggled up the roller coaster track, for it was suddenly much slipperier than before.

"Almost there!" Philby called from the top.

The next scene looked like Yellowstone Park. Geysers spit into the air. There were pools of water in luminous shades of green and yellow.

The ground beneath them shook. Philby touched the rail to see if it was vibrating, meaning that the ride had turned itself on. He shook his head.

"Maybe it's just an effect. You know: Yellowstone. Earthquakes and stuff like that."

"I'd have read about that," Philby declared. "I don't think so."

The ground shook even more furiously, and now Finn was scared. Too much weird stuff had happened on the rides for him not to be afraid.

A few yards down the track, Finn felt the first touch of cold creep into his legs.

"Philby!"

"Yeah, I feel it too," Philby answered.

With his legs going numb, Finn found it hard to walk. He whispered, "The only time we've felt this before—"

"Maleficent," Philby answered.

"Yeah."

Water at the top of the geysers turned first to ice and then snow, which fell thickly.

Finn's cold legs were nearly impossible to move. "We've got to get out of here!" He could feel the chill seeping into his chest, his breathing tight and difficult. Too much longer, and he wouldn't be going anywhere.

Philby stopped them both and said, "Listen to that!"

Like something cracking apart, Finn thought. Ice? It didn't sound exactly like ice.

"We've got to hurry!" Philby barked out.

"Hurry? I can barely move."

The cracking sound grew frighteningly loud. It

came from the scene behind them—the Utah desert scene they'd just left.

They cautiously climbed back up the small rise in the track, to look back from where they'd just come. They peered over the rails, following that loud cracking sound.

Across the way, rock splintered around the enormous dinosaur fossil.

"That's a T. rex," Philby whispered. "Forty feet long. Eighteen feet high. Fifty-eight teeth. Runs forty miles an hour."

Finn didn't need all the facts. Sometimes he wished Philby would just keep them to himself.

The two boys watched in horror as, one by one, the bones vibrated and broke free from the rock. They did not fall. They did not break. They held together as one . . . giant . . .

"Run!" Philby shouted.

A cloud of dust rose behind them as the ground trembled with a rhythmic *clomp, clomp, clomp.*

Footsteps. *Big* footsteps.

All at once, the T. rex skeleton came over the hill, following the tracks. The thing was *huge.*

The dinosaur had all its bones, with no eyes, no skin, no flesh—but *all* its teeth.

Philby shouted, "Keep running! Don't slow down!"

Finn's cold, unwilling legs slowed him. He scrambled ahead. The T. rex charged, lowering its head and coming for them. Finn was behind Philby, close to the charge.

Clomp! Clomp! Clomp!

The ground shook so violently that Finn fell. He slid down the rails, caught hold, and regained his balance.

The bones clattered as the dinosaur charged. The boys climbed the next rise and jumped over. The beast moved faster.

Finn made a mistake by glancing back. The beast snorted dust out of the holes in its skull where nostrils should have been. It lowered its head once again and picked up speed, the jaws clapping open and shut, sounding like a door being slammed.

Finn cleared the top of the roller coaster's next rocky peak, with the dinosaur's jaw bones snapping only a few feet from him now. Finn was going to be eaten. He slid down the last descending slope of the roller coaster, as if he were sliding down an enormous banister.

The track leveled off here, giving the dinosaur the advantage. It snapped and caught a piece of Finn's shirt.

The track curved ahead. Finn, finding speed he didn't know he had, cried, "Help!"

"Physics class!" shouted Philby back at him. "The track is *banked*."

"What do I care?"

The T. rex stumbled and lost a few yards. The boys hurried up the slight rise into the steep turn.

"The track is *banked*!" Philby repeated.

Finn understood then what had to be done. He was the one trailing. His heart lodged in his throat as he stopped just before the apex of the turn. He faced the beast, making a target of himself.

"Come and get it!" he shouted at the T. rex.

He waved his arms like a matador taunting the bull.

The huge mass of rattling bones, surrounded by a cloud of dust, bore down on him. Faster and faster it came.

Finn waited . . . and waited . . . knowing he had to time his move perfectly.

The T. rex charged.

Just as the skeleton's teeth were a foot away from his chest, Finn dove off the track.

The beast faltered, lurched, and tipped to its left when the track suddenly curved to the right. The bones of an outer leg splintered and snapped at the knee. The monster rolled, broke through the plywood of the scene's mountain backdrop, and tumbled over the side.

Finn watched as it landed with a noisy explosion of broken bones that scattered like tree branches.

Philby, who had also stopped, looked down at Finn and helped him up to the rail.

"Wait till they see that on their cameras!"

The boys turned and hurried off into the night.

Since all of the kids were hungry, they left the apartment together and reconvened at Cosmic Ray's Starlight Cafe. Finn led the way, passing right through the locked front door.

Maybeck surprised the others by cooking up decent-tasting turkey burgers. They stayed in the kitchen area and kept the lights off so as not to be seen. Exit signs and a few overhead security lights provided the only illumination. Finn and Philby fashioned a table out of a rolling cart with locking wheels. Inverted plastic tubs and buckets served as chairs. The two girls sat together on one side, Finn and Philby on the other. Maybeck joined them last and took the head of the table.

Philby placed a paper napkin in front of them.

"This is everything we have," he explained, jotting down the letters they'd acquired by following the clues in the fable:

FMEYIRSTPN

"They must spell something," Charlene said.

"If I was at a computer . . . If I had an anagram generator," Philby said.

He wrote the letters out again, this time leaving more room around each one. He tore the letters apart. A few minutes later they had Scrabble letters made out of a torn napkin.

The kids studied the letters, calling out words they saw.

"MEN," Charlene said.

"Leave that to you!" Willa quipped.

Philby set the letters aside.

Finn said, "SPIT."

He pulled these out as well.

"FRY is left," Philby pointed out.

"MEN FRY SPIT?" Willa asked.

"MEN SPIT FRY?" Charlene suggested.

"No way," Philby said. "We'll try again." He reshuffled the ten letters.

E

N   P

S   T   M

Y   F   R   I

"I'm killer at Scrabble," Charlene announced, "if I do say so myself."

"Have at it," Philby said.

Charlene arranged the letters into groups, broke up those groups and tried again. Her hands moved very fast, like a card dealer.

She assembled them into:

MY PIT FERNS.

"Very good!" Willa said encouragingly.

MY TIP FERNS

"Again," Philby said. Finn kept track, writing down all the variations.

FIRM SPY NET

"That's an interesting one," Philby said.

Finn made sure to get it down.

MEN FIST PRY

"You *are* good at this!" Willa said, impressed.

"We all have our talents," Charlene quipped.

Then, two right in a row:

MET FRY SPIN, MY PINS FRET.

Suddenly Maybeck sneezed, sending the letters airborne. Finn and Philby snagged a few of them and returned them to the table.

Others floated down like large snowflakes. They settled, one by one.

"Wait!" Finn called out. He gasped as he saw what the letters were spelling all by themselves:

W Y

F IR S T

P EN

Finn licked the tip of his finger, touched the *W* and turned it over. He then neatened the rest:

"The Stonecutter's *Quill*. It's Walt Disney's first pen," Philby said. "Oh my gosh!"

"But what does it mean?" Charlene said.

"It's the next clue. It means we've got to find Walt's first pen," Philby answered.

Maybeck groaned, "You have got to be kidding me."

"But where?" Charlene asked.

Silence.

"Is there a museum or something?" Finn asked.

The kids all shook their heads.

"There's that thing, One Man's Dream," Willa stated. "Over in Disney-MGM. It's kind of like a museum, I suppose."

Philby said, "That sounds . . . relevant."

"What are you, a lawyer?" Maybeck said.

Willa continued, "As I remember, there's stuff there, like an old desk and models and things like that."

"Worth a try," Finn muttered softly.

"Wayne," Philby said, drawing everyone's attention. "This is a question for Wayne."

Maybeck said, "I paid him a visit. Asked him to join us in the apartment. He said his hip was bothering him, and that if we wanted to see him, it would have to be at his place."

"Well, then," Finn said. "I guess that's that."

They split up into two groups—Finn with Willa; Maybeck and Philby with Charlene—and left the restaurant five minutes apart.

The area of greatest risk was Main Street, which was the park's sole entrance and exit. You couldn't leave or enter the Magic Kingdom without walking down Main Street. The fire station was up at Town Square, at the opposite end of the street from where they were.

When Finn and Willa reached the park end of Main Street—the area near the castle—they stayed close to the storefronts, ducking into doorways and sneaking glances out onto the empty street. Twice they hid in the shadows against a door as Finn spotted the taillights of golf carts in the distance. He checked his watch: in two minutes the other three would leave the restaurant. The idea had been for Finn and Willa to be safely inside Wayne's by then.

The most risk came with crossing the street. Finn signaled to Willa and counted down with his fingers. *Three . . . two . . . one . . .*

They took off across the street, two blurs of dull, colorful light. As they did, Finn had the pronounced feeling that someone was watching him. He glanced over his shoulder and thought he saw a shadow move in one of the doorways. But who?

Door to door they moved up Main Street. Finn

looked back, but there was no more sign of anyone following. When he was sure they were in the clear, he led Willa toward the fire station and up the back stairs. Wayne answered the door as if he'd been waiting for them.

"I think you've done it," Wayne said, with all five DHIs gathered in his apartment. Philby and Finn had explained their solution to the fable.

Wayne continued, "It was the glasses, you see? That reference to perspective was where we failed all these years. You should be very proud of yourselves."

"Is that it?" Maybeck asked. "Can we start sleeping again, for real?"

"You can try," Wayne answered, "but I'm willing to think you'll have to see it through."

"See *what* through?" Maybeck complained. "You wanted us to solve the fable, and we did."

Wayne stared at Finn until the boy said, "It's not solved. Maybe the pen is the end of it."

"It's possible," Wayne said, "but I wouldn't count on it."

"Why can't you take it from here?" Maybeck asked.

"I could try," Wayne answered. "But I'm not sure that would solve your crossing-over problem."

"You designed us to cross over. So *un*-design us," Charlene said.

"If only it were that easy. No, I'm afraid Finn's right: you'll need to see this through."

"You're after *her*," Maybeck said, finally understanding. "Was this ever about the fable? Or is that just a way to smoke her out?"

"It's very much about the fable," Wayne answered. "I sense some hostility in you, Terry."

"Do you really?" Maybeck snorted and crossed his arms. "That wouldn't be because I was kidnapped, would it? And now you want me coming back for *more*?"

Willa asked, "Is he right? Are we supposed to . . . deliver . . . that *thing*. Maleficent? How do we do that?"

"You take things one at a time," Wayne replied. "Let's not get ahead of ourselves."

"One Man's Dream," Finn said.

"You can go in as a DHI, but you won't get out with what you want," Wayne stated, surprising them. "Think about it. You might get inside, but the pen would not come out with you. The pen is material and real, whereas you—"

"Are not," Philby answered.

"So we have to steal it?" Finn asked.

"You are going to borrow it, I suppose."

"Why can't *you* do that?" Maybeck challenged.

"I wasn't the one to solve the fable. I'm not the

one brought here to fix things. You are. All five of you."

"But you could get the pen if you wanted."

"Could I? If an old goat like me from Imagineering asked to get inside a display in One Man's Dream, they'd probably fire me. I have no business there."

"Which display?" Philby asked. "You know which display, don't you?"

"I have an idea," Wayne admitted.

"Sheesh!" Maybeck huffed, fed up.

"There are several replicas. A drafting table. His school desk. Even Walt's original office. A pen . . . it's conceivable it could be in any of these. You must bring me the pen the moment you have it. And understand the threat you now pose to the Overtakers. Don't underestimate that. Not for a minute. You've solved the fable. They may know that, or at least suspect it. If the pen is valuable enough, powerful enough, to hide inside a fable, then one can imagine we are not the only ones after it."

"You're afraid of her," Willa said softly. "You created us because you're afraid of her."

"Are you old enough to understand the saying: 'Don't shoot the messenger'?" Wayne asked.

Finn had heard the expression before, and judging by the faces of the others, they had too. He thought he understood Wayne's message. "You're not the one who created us," he said. "So who did?"

Voices came loudly up the back stairs from outside. Several men. One of them said, "Was this where you saw them?"

"We were spotted!" Charlene said in a panic.

"You'll have to go now," Wayne said.

He looked toward Finn, who said in a panicked voice, "The remote's back in the apartment. That's where we leave it!"

The sound of feet coming up the stairs grew all the louder.

A pounding on the back door.

Wayne had a contented smile on his face. "You don't think we'd do this without making a backup, do you?" he said, holding up an exact replica of their remote.

Another loud knock on the door. "Open up, please!" a deep male voice commanded.

"Gather 'round," Wayne said, calm and relaxed, as if he had not a care in the world.

The DHIs huddled together.

Wayne pushed the button.

The Transportation and Ticket Center hummed with conversation as a tangle of park visitors shuttled between buses and monorails. Some families were ending their days just as others were starting theirs. On a Monday afternoon, thick with humidity, the tired and impatient mingled with the exhilarated and anxious. For some, a day spent; for others, an evening full of promise. The humidity hung in the air so heavily you could practically wear it like a coat.

Above the giggles and shrieks of excited children and the scornful reproaches of their exhausted parents, the purr of a train approaching could be heard.

"We're off to a late start," Philby announced, checking his watch. Charlene's cheerleader practice had delayed them. "It's almost a quarter to five."

"One Man's Dream closes at five," Willa informed them. "We're okay. We'll make it." She turned to Finn. "What if we were 'accidentally' inside when it closed for the night?"

Philby shot down her suggestion. "There's no way five of us will be able to hide out in there and get locked in. Forget it."

Finn said, "But one of us might be able to."

Philby said, "There are at least nine security cameras inside One Man's Dream. If even one of us is seen in there after closing, we're in big trouble."

"Maybe not." A familiar voice came from behind Finn. It was Amanda.

She was sitting in the front part of the train car, her back directly to them, exactly behind Finn. This is anything but coincidence, he thought.

Finn had barely spoken to her since that day at the skate park where it had seemed to him she'd known too much, or was keeping something from him. His intentional avoidance of her hung in the air between them.

Finn introduced her around to those who had not met her.

She told Finn candidly, "You saw me in the park last night. Main Street. Not far behind you." The four other DHIs looked at Finn as if he'd betrayed them. "That's because I followed Jez there after school," Amanda explained.

"Jez?" Maybeck blurted out.

Amanda said, "Jez never left the park at closing. She went into Pirates of the Caribbean and never came out. I hid in the bathrooms behind Pirates and waited for the park to clear. Then I hid in a stairwell and waited."

"Are we supposed to believe this?" Charlene asked.

"Believe what you want," Amanda snapped at her. "After closing, it was her turn to hide. She took a place on Main Street. You guys just . . . arrived all of a sudden. I mean, one minute no one was there on the bench, and then there you were. It was the *weirdest* thing. And she followed you."

"And you followed her," Finn said.

Philby tested her. "She followed us where?"

Amanda answered, "She followed you and Finn to Thunder Mountain, and so did I."

Maybeck nodded. What he heard made sense. "This is solid, guys. This girl Jez is trouble."

"Later she went over to Cosmic Ray's," Amanda said.

Charlene went pale. "But why?"

"Yeah. Why would Jez follow us?" Philby asked curiously.

Amanda said, "Curiosity killed the cat."

Finn and Maybeck exchanged glances. Finn asked, "Where is she now?"

"She followed you, Finn, today. After school. I lost her at the Transportation and Ticket Center, but she's around here someplace."

Charlene snapped, "Since when did you become our guardian angel?"

"My mother works at MGM," Amanda said. "In

administration, in one of the old bungalows. I've been there, like, a zillion times. They know me. The main security office for the park is in that building." She hesitated a moment and then said, "I know those guys. I can distract them. If I think they're going to see you on one of their screens, I can draw their attention."

"I'll just bet you can," snarled Charlene.

"I don't know about that," Finn said. It sounded complicated to him. Risky.

"I can help you," she suggested. "I can signal if they're on to you." Still Finn hesitated. "You need someone to warn you."

He'd known for some time that she wanted to be a DHI, wanted to be part of the adventure.

Showing off her knowledge of the area, Amanda told Philby, "Listen, there's a sound-and-light tower right there at the side door to One Man's Dream. From up there, one of you would be able to see pretty much all around the park. You'd be able to spot the security patrols way before they reached the attraction."

Willa suggested, "All in favor of Amanda helping us out?"

Everyone's hand went up, but Finn's was noticeably slower than the others. Noting his reluctance, Amanda scrunched her face at him.

"I just don't want you getting into trouble—or

worse!—for something you're not involved in," he said. "This can be dangerous, Amanda. You need to know that before you volunteer."

Amanda's nostrils flared. She looked angry. "I can take care of myself."

Willa and Charlene grinned.

Charlene, usually the most reluctant of the five, said, "Okay then, it's decided."

Once inside MGM park, they quickly split up to avoid recognition.

Finn and Willa headed up Sunset Boulevard. Amanda split from the group, presumably to reach Security. Philby sought out the sound-and-light tower, with Charlene as his runner, in case he spotted trouble.

"You don't look so hot," Willa told Finn.

"I'm just . . . nervous, I guess," Finn said. They had come up with a decent plan on how he might hide inside One Man's Dream, but he wasn't eager to test it.

He asked, "What if they count heads? What if they know how many go in and out of the theater?"

Willa considered this and then said, "Nah, they don't do stuff like that. Maybe they count people going into the park, but not onto the rides. That doesn't make sense."

"They might."

"They might, but they don't."

The two passed the fifty-foot-high replica of Mickey's sorcerer hat that stood in front of the Chinese theater and served as a bandstand. They stopped at a kiosk selling pins and film, hats, stuffed animals, and postcards.

One Man's Dream was crowded with grandparents and mothers with strollers trying to escape the muggy heat. Finn passed several displays dealing with the history of the park and the ways in which the Imagineers had realized Walt Disney's dream. Willa waited near the entrance, doing a good imitation of a girl waiting for a friend.

One of the displays showed Walt Disney's second-grade school desk from Marceline, Missouri. Finn studied the desk carefully, wondering if Disney's "first pen" might be inside. Its wooden top was hinged, with a shallow circular well cut into it for a bottle of ink.

"Not exactly like your desk at school, I'll bet," said a woman standing behind Finn. She was very old, with kind eyes, translucent skin, and a faint white moustache. She wore an employee name tag that said CHARLOTTE. Her hair was the color of laundry lint. Her eyelashes were so pale they were almost invisible, which left her eyelids looking like weird flesh-colored cups that blinked down over her eyes like a bird's.

Her voice sounded like the squeal of a pinched balloon.

Finn, who'd hoped to go through the exhibit unnoticed, blurted out, "I—it—didn't do anything."

"I didn't say you did, young man." She looked at him curiously.

"Am I too late to watch the movie on Walt Disney's life?"

"No, not at all. There's a final showing in . . ." She checked her watch. "Well! You'll have to hurry. It's just down the hall and to your right. It's biographical, you understand? It's not like the Bug movie or PhilharMagic. Nothing like those."

"I know," Finn said. The woman's heavy perfume made him dizzy. It trailed after her like car exhaust. She apparently felt obliged to make sure he made it in time. Together they walked past other displays. Finn caught sight of Walt Disney's West Coast office—the display Wayne had mentioned.

"Here we go, young man," the woman said. "Wait here and they'll show you inside."

Finn saw another display, this one open to the air, not sealed under glass: a drafting table with a bunch of pens and papers. Wayne had mentioned this as well. Which display? Finn wondered.

The doors to the theater opened. Finn and a few

others were shown inside. Finn took a seat near the back.

The lights dimmed almost immediately and the film started. Finn watched a few minutes of it, slouched down in his seat, and then slipped onto the floor. He curled up tightly under the seat in front of him in order to hide. The film ran about fifteen minutes. Finn was already feeling stiff by the time it finished.

The theatergoers exited into daylight. Finn's heart raced in his chest as he hid and the doors to the outside thumped shut, closing him in. The theater darkened. More sounds: ushers making small talk, people saying good-bye and good night.

Then silence.

Finn, still on the floor, uncoiled and relaxed his tight muscles. Two minutes passed. Five. No sounds at all beyond the almost painful beating of his heart.

He got to his feet, gathered his courage, and called out, "Hello?" prepared to invent some excuse if he raised anyone.

Nothing.

He pushed through the doors and walked back into the main gallery. He tried once more: "Hello?" If discovered, he'd claim he had fallen asleep during the film.

Nothing.

A few lights had been left on, but the ones inside the displays were all off. Finn checked out the drafting table. He was disappointed to read the little sign that described the display. There was no mention of the drafting table having belonged to Walt Disney. It was just one of many drafting tables used by his animation staff. There were a couple pens and pencils, a clear plastic draftsman's triangle, and some papers scattered around. Finn carefully climbed into the display and opened some small drawers of a cabinet next to the table. All empty.

Next, he returned to the display of Walt Disney's original office. There on the desk, both a mug and a cork globe held an abundance of pens and pencils. A dozen or more. *My first pen.* Finn knew just by looking that this was the place.

He didn't want to *steal* anything. He reminded himself that this had been Wayne's idea, not his. They were *borrowing* the pens. Nothing more. Wayne could return them. No harm.

But how to get inside the glassed-in display? Finn didn't see any kind of door, except the one leading into the office, and it was in the back wall of the display. He saw no way in.

He searched for a possible access door into the back of the displays, assuming there was a hallway behind the various windows. The only door he found, toward the main entrance, was not only locked but far away from the office display.

He backtracked, passing all the displays again. He found no door. No way back there. But there had to be a way! Some way to move furniture, dust, clean, change lightbulbs.

Only as he passed a blue poster for the third time did he happen to notice a small floor-to-ceiling gap. The poster was a sketch of the earth with Mickey Mouse ears. The earth was crying. The small description explained that this drawing had been a newspaper cartoon that ran following Disney's death. It depicted the world mourning his loss.

Finn shoved his fingers into the small crack and pulled. The poster moved and the door came open. He was inside in an instant.

Just as he stepped into relative darkness behind the door, Finn heard three loud knocks at a distance. Willa's signal. Terror flooded him. Security guards were either in the area or headed for One Man's Dream. Five knocks would signal that the coast was clear. He pulled the door shut behind him. This was as good a place to hide as any.

A moment later he stood absolutely still as he identified deep voices nearby. Just through the wall. Two men talking. *Inside* the attraction.

"You say it was an anonymous call?" One guard speaking to another.

"A girl. Young girl at that," the other said. "That's what Manny said, yeah. Probably just a prank. You know kids that age. But if Manny wants it checked out . . ."

"Then we check it out."

"Got that right."

Finn held his breath as they drew close.

"Thing is," the second guard said, "the front door was locked good and tight. We check the other doors and we got nothing to worry about. No way someone's in here if all the doors are tight. False alarm. Plain and simple. Am I right?"

"You're right."

"Okay, then let's get some coffee."

"I'm all over that."

Finn waited several more long minutes without moving, practically without breathing. Who had called security? Amanda? Had she fed them a bunch of lies? Did she *want* Finn to get caught because of the way he'd excluded her recently?

If they were caught now, their attempt to stop Maleficent would be thwarted. The park would eventually fall under her control. Worse, if she took her powers outside the park, who knew what would happen?

Who knew what would become of the five kids who had once been DHIs?

One anonymous call had nearly ruined everything.

Now he heard a distant sound: five dull beats, like a fist on glass. The signal.

His eyes adjusted to what little light was available in this back hallway. He turned left toward the office display and soon reached a door marked: WD'S OFFICE.

Finn opened this door, stepped inside, and was now standing in the display. He moved carefully, not wanting to nudge anything out of place or disturb the office's contents. The air was stuffy and unusually dry. He kept watch out into the empty gallery beyond.

On the wall a tiny red light began flashing. A sensor of some kind, though an alarm did not sound. An environmental sensor perhaps, measuring heat and humidity for the sake of the display's contents. Finn's body heat and his breathing, along with the open door to the back hall, had tripped some kind of silent alarm.

He quickly snatched up all the pens and pencils from both the black coffee mug and the cork globe. He was nearly out the office door when he saw a scroll of architectural plans leaning up against the desk. Walt had told Wayne that he "had plans for this place." Finn, like Wayne and others, had taken the wrong meaning. *Plans*, as in drawings, not *plans*, as in ideas. Finn scooped them up.

He heard three loud thuds on the gallery's outer door—another signal from Willa. Someone was coming. Again.

Finn hurried out the office's back door, shut it carefully, and headed down the back hallway.

But where to go? he wondered.

He saw an exit sign at either end of the hallway. Which way?

He looked left, looked right, but was frozen by indecision.

He headed right, away from Willa's warning.

Down the narrow hall, a jog left, he faced a metal exit door with a panic bar. He hesitated, for at that very second an icy frost splintered and cracked the inside surface of the door. Something—*someone*—was just on the other side, and it wasn't security guards.

The frosty image slowly took the shape of a human hand. Finn jumped back. He could see his breath now, could feel that same penetrating cold getting to him again.

He turned to run, but could not move his legs. He teetered, ready to fall. The frost on the inside of the door spread from the thin fingers of the hand like a web. Finn glanced down to see that the floor had iced up beneath him. It was like standing on a skating rink. Then his body moved forward, all on its own, sliding on the ice, as if drawn by a magnet.

He put out his hands to stop himself, but they stuck to the door. That force continued to pull him. Now his body glued itself to the door. Inch by inch his head was pulled until his cheek froze to the metal. Pulled against the door's panic bar, he feared the door might come open. Whoever, whatever, was on the other side wanted the pens and pencils in his pocket. The Overtakers.

The plans squirted out from under his arm and came unrolled as they hit the floor. Finn could see they were faded blueprints of the various parks. One by one, the sheets slipped under the door while Finn was helpless to stop them.

The panic bar inched ahead and, as it did, the mechanism drew the bolt of the lock away from the lip of metal that secured the door shut.

Behind him, the voices inside the gallery grew louder as the security guards drew closer. "Hey, Manny! Over here! Think I got something!"

The guards were in the back hallway.

Whatever was on the other side of the door made a sound like wintry wind.

Finn tried to dismiss it, ignore it, but it grew louder.

Then, from outside the door, Finn heard shouting. The roar of the wind immediately lessened, fading away, replaced by the sounds of running feet. The ice on the inside of the door slowly melted, sending streams of water rushing down.

Finn heard the slap of boots as the security guards drew closer. He pushed the panic bar. The ice cracked and the door opened. Finn tore some skin off the palms of both hands as he pulled away from the icy bar.

Bright late-afternoon sunshine blinded him. He could just vaguely make out Willa, a good distance away, running toward him.

Behind him, a girl with long hair.

Jez? Amanda?

Finn took off in that direction, curious to find out who had caused that ice.

The fleeing girl rounded the building's back corner, out of sight.

Finn sprinted to catch up calling, "Hey! Wait! You! Wait up!" He was no longer afraid of this person. He wanted answers.

He, too, hurried around the corner. He collided with someone and they went down hard. Finn came to his knees, dazed.

"You?" he said.

He sat face-to-face with Amanda.

"You?" he said again, desperate for an explanation. "*You* cause the cold?"

"Finn—"

"You're the one?" he gasped in disbelief, hating her for all her lies.

"Me?" She looked astonished. But was she just acting?

She said in a whisper, "Did you get what you came for?"

Finn couldn't get a word out, his chest tight, his fists clenched.

"Finn, please. You've got this wrong."

He rose to his feet and backed away from her, but not daring to take his eyes off her. "I trusted you," he said.

"Finn," she pleaded. "There's so much to explain. But not here."

"Not anywhere," he fired back. "Not ever."

"Run!" Willa called out, catching up. "They're coming!"

Amanda, still seated on the pavement, had tears in her eyes.

Willa came to a breathless stop. "Finn! The guards!"

He and Amanda had not broken eye contact, though they did now. He backed up at first, still looking at her. Then he turned and ran as hard and as fast as he could.

Mickey's Not-So-Scary Halloween Party, the most fun of any of the park's special events, was not to be missed. It provided a good opportunity for the kids to bring the pens to Wayne, since they would have to deliver them in person, not as DHIs.

All five of the kids had planned to attend, using up one of their "legal" visits to the park. Finn wasn't sure who to trust anymore, but certainly not the pirates. Their apparent connection to Jez made him all the more curious, and all the more cautious.

The party took place at night, after hours. Main Street was decorated to match the occasion, costumes were all but mandatory, and ghoulish characters walked the streets, adding to the chills and thrills.

Philby believed the party also provided Maleficent a rare opportunity to use all the costuming to hide herself. A witch would go unnoticed on a night like this. She could meet with the other Overtakers without raising an eyebrow, and could move about the park freely. If she was plotting a way to take over the park, this, of all nights, seemed the perfect time for her to spring her plan.

The kids—kids, not DHIs—had a plan in place to keep both Pirates of the Caribbean and the Haunted Mansion under close watch. They chose the Haunted Mansion because ghosts and goblins would serve a witch well, and if Maleficent planned to take over the park, now or in the future, she would need an army of Overtakers supporting her.

Finn's mother dropped him off in the school parking lot. He suffered through the usual lecture from her about good and proper behavior. Snore. Over three hundred of his fellow schoolmates, including Dillard, rode school bus shuttles to the Magic Kingdom. These same buses were to take them all back to the school at eleven o'clock, when the party ended and the park closed. Parents would pick up their kids in the school's lot.

Once inside, the plan was for the kids to meet at the statue of Roy O. Disney outside the fire station in Town Square. From there they would "divide and conquer," as Maybeck put it.

Having struggled with costume ideas, Finn came dressed in black jeans, a black T-shirt, and a new cape. He wore a black mask over just his eyes. He thought of himself as Zorro, when in truth, he was dressed for any adventures they might encounter.

At eight o'clock thousands of kids and their families poured into the park wearing elaborate costumes that added to the heightened sense of fun. In any other year, Finn would have headed straight to a ride to get in line, ready to scream and be frightened. Despite its name, Mickey's Not-So-Scary Halloween Party offered plenty of frights to its guests.

Music was pumped into the park, not the typical Disney songs—most of which Finn could hum from memory—but instead, monster tunes and ghost songs, punctuated by fits of ghoulish laughter. The park came alive with the sounds.

Arriving as planned, a few minutes past opening, Finn found it difficult to pick out his new friends. This was partly because there were so many people flooding into the park, and partly because of the costumes.

"There you are!" Dillard Cole said. He'd elected to come as a crab, wearing a large round shell made of brown paper, his hands in oven mitts for claws, and several sets of springy legs protruding from the shell.

"You look like a giant tick," Finn said. "Crabs aren't brown."

"Grocery bags. It was the only paper we could find."

From up close, Finn saw that Dillard's costume was indeed made from dozens of grocery bags cut open and taped together.

"You seen anyone from school?" Finn asked.

"Nah. You?"

"Nah."

"I hate Halloween," Dillard said.

"Then why did you come?"

The crab shrugged, all its legs bouncing at once. "The candy. Where you been, anyway? Seems like we never hang out anymore."

It was true: Finn's life had changed since the crossing-over had begun. He'd quickly made new friends with the DHIs. Their quest was all he thought of anymore; even his homework was suffering.

"You know what's going on," he said. "Or at least some of it."

"Your *super powers*," Dillard teased.

"Yeah. Like that." Finn hadn't told Dillard half the stuff he'd been through in the past few weeks. He led a secret life now.

Until this moment he hadn't realized just how secret. Worse: until he and the others fixed things, until the growing power of the Overtakers was challenged and stopped, his life wasn't going to get much better. Staying awake all night. Feeling tired all day. Battling his parents. Telling his mom the truth, which she, of course, found unbelievable.

"What ride do you want to go on first?" Dillard asked. "Earth to Finn! Hello?"

Finn couldn't hear because he'd spotted a witch heading for them. Among all the other costumes, this one in particular stood out. Not just for the costume, but for the girl who wore it.

As Dillard turned to follow Finn's gaze, his crab body and legs hit kids behind him, drawing jeers of complaint and clearing a space around him.

"Check out Cruella De Vil," Dillard said, following Finn's gaze. "Hey, isn't that—"

"Her name is Jez."

"From the car wash."

"Right."

Jez wore a skintight black-and-white leotard with black-and-white tights. Her hair was half black, half white. She carried a masquerade mask on a stick and wore white gloves that ran all the way up to her elbows. The small mask was black, like Finn's Zorro mask. She had a black beauty mark drawn onto her cheek to the left of her lips, which were exaggerated by bright red lipstick. She looked like a college girl. Her cape swished dramatically as she walked. It wasn't made of cheap costume material, but something much nicer. She drew looks from a good number of boys as she passed.

She headed directly to Finn and Dillard. The song playing from the bushes was "Monster Mash." Jez stepped up to Finn, standing a little too close. They almost touched. Finn felt tempted to take a step back, but held his ground.

Jez spoke softly, privately. "Great minds think alike," she said. "Our masks," she added after Finn failed to respond.

"Hey, Jez," Finn said.

"Look out, Zorro," she warned, "I might put a spell on you!" She briefly dropped the mask and met eyes with Finn. She smiled.

Dillard coughed. A coughing crab with dancing legs. He cleared an even bigger space for himself in the crowd.

"Maybe you already have," Finn suggested.

She said, "A good spell, I hope."

"Are you a good witch?"

"The best," she said. "Can't you tell?" She spun, her cape rising. She ended her twirl facing Dillard and said to him, "Aren't you going to offer to get me something to drink, Sebastian?"

"Hey! She guessed I'm Sebastian!" Dillard said proudly to Finn.

"You've got enough hands, don't you?" she asked, tweaking one claw and sending it bouncing up and down.

Finn said, "He's not an errand boy, he's my friend."

"Hey! I don't mind," Dillard said. He raised his oven mitts, made claw motions, and waddled off in search of something for them to drink.

"He's a good guy," Finn said, when Jez faced him again. "He's big, so people make fun of him, but he can't help it."

She ignored what he'd said. "Want to do the Haunted Mansion with me?" Jez asked.

Finn felt his throat tighten in panic. The mansion was an attraction that seemed perfect to hide Overtakers. "It'll be too crowded," he said.

An awkward moment settled between them.

"*Miss Congeniality*," Finn said.

"What?"

"The Sandra Bullock movie?" Finn inquired. He pointed toward the park entrance. "A friend of mine . . . Charlene. You met her at the sports park," he said. Charlene also wore makeup and lipstick, which gave her high cheekbones and a thinner face. It was a good disguise. Her blue cocktail dress swished as she paraded straight over to Finn.

Charlene looked Jez up and down. "Adorable," she said insincerely.

"Imaginative," Jez said back to her.

Charlene ignored Jez. "Sorry if I'm *late*," she said.

"No prob."

"Finn and I are going over to the Haunted Mansion," Jez announced. "Want to come?"

Charlene complained, "But Finn, you promised me the first ride. *Remember*, Finn?"

She was giving him the excuse they needed to get over to Pirates and be with the others.

"When you're right, you're right!" Finn said, a little awkwardly. He asked Jez if he could catch up to her later for the Haunted Mansion.

She frowned.

Dillard returned, bearing too many drinks to hold. He dropped one.

Jez reached out and caught it as it fell. She not only snagged the cup but somehow managed to catch all the soda as well. Not a drop spilled to the ground. It was an impossible feat.

Finn took a moment to replay it in his mind. "How did you *do* that?"

Charlene took the third cup from Dillard and thanked him.

"I . . . ahh . . ." Jez said.

Dillard had intended one of the three for himself, but didn't tell that to Charlene. When he moved, his various arms bounced wildly. He mumbled and headed off to get another.

"You didn't answer me," Finn reminded Jez. "How did you do that?"

Jez stumbled over her words as she made what

was clearly a lame excuse. "My mom doesn't like me messing up the kitchen. I've gotten pretty good at not spilling."

Catwoman approached. Finn recognized Amanda immediately.

Finn hadn't spoken to her since their collision behind One Man's Dream. He couldn't sort everything out: what she'd been doing there; why the cold hadn't seemed to affect her. He didn't feel like hanging out with her tonight. He wasn't sure how to tell her.

Dillard returned fairly quickly and said hello to Amanda. Her attention remained on Finn.

"Finn?" Amanda said.

Finn turned his back, not sure what to do. Not that, he realized, as she stormed off. He felt rotten.

Finn offered Charlene and Jez another drink and then headed off himself, grateful to get away. The girls hung with Dillard, who struggled to get a paper cup to his mouth. He spilled some soda down his front when one of his own claws banged against him.

Amanda snuck up behind Finn in the soda line.

"I saw her, Finn. Jez. Behind One Man's Dream. Those monitors are old and fuzzy, but I'm sure it was her, and I came over there to warn you."

Again, Finn didn't know what to say, didn't know what to think. He didn't turn around.

Amanda continued, "Doesn't that strike you as a little odd? A little too coincidental, her being there like that? Right then?"

"You were there, too. That struck me as odd as well."

"I just explained."

They stepped away from the soda line. Finn juggled three cups. "You weren't sure it was her. You just said so yourself."

"Think about her name, Finn. Jezebel? Come on. The Bible?"

He was not exactly a Bible scholar.

"Jezebel is wicked. Evil. Just like a witch. And that fits with the cold, right?" Amanda asked.

"It could have been anyone doing that," Finn blurted out, thinking of the woman in the car.

She leaned back and looked at him as if she didn't know him. "What are you thinking? Are you *serious?* Me? Listen, there's something you need to hear . . . something I have to tell you about her. I'm not supposed to—do you understand that? This could get me in big trouble. . . ."

Suddenly, Amanda shuddered. Her head jerked up toward the sky. Her shoulders shrugged and stiffened. Her eyes rolled in her head. Finn thought she was going to faint. He dumped all the drinks into a nearby trash can, freeing his hands, and took her by the arm. Then by the waist. She sank into his arms. She felt cold, really cold, and stiff, as if she were suffering some kind of seizure.

Finn, wanting to avoid making a scene, walked her to a bench and sat her down.

A commotion erupted behind him. He turned to see Charlene now sitting down on the sidewalk, her head hanging slack over her knees. She had apparently fainted as well.

An adult hurried toward Charlene.

"Finn!" It was Willa, late to arrive.

"No time to explain," he said. "You've got to get Charlene over here before people start asking questions. The giant crab—that's Dillard—he'll help you. Hurry!"

Willa, who'd come as Dorothy from the Wizard of Oz, rushed across to Dillard, took hold of one of his oven mitts, and dragged him over to the wilted Charlene.

Finn checked Amanda. She looked half asleep, her eyes barely open. Thankfully, she was breathing normally. "Amanda!" he said, but got nothing from her.

A brownout, he thought. But a brownout affecting a human, not a DHI.

If you're not careful, I'll cast a spell on you. Hadn't Jez said something like that? Was he imagining that she'd said that?

He looked around, his eyes searching for Jez.

Hadn't Amanda been just about to tell him something to do with Jez when she'd fainted?

Willa and Dillard had Charlene walking between them. Definitely a good sign.

There! Finn finally spotted Jez. She stood on the far side of the street, talking to an adult—a thin woman in a large witch's hat, her back to Finn. He watched as Jez pointed in his direction. He felt goosebumps race up his spine. What was she talking about?

Then, just for an instant, Jez accidentally met eyes with Finn, from clear across the street. A moment later Jez led the woman off, absorbed by the crowd.

"Listen . . . Finn said, trying to think. "I gotta go," he told Willa.

"What, just leave us here?" Willa asked, astonished.

"You know anything about the Bible?" he asked Willa.

"A little. Sure."

"I think I know what's going on," he announced to Willa just as Philby and Maybeck showed up.

"I'm glad someone does," Maybeck said.

Philby had come wearing a white curly wig and big black glasses, calling himself Einstein. Maybeck had sprayed his hair gray and wore the flag of South Africa on his sleeve.

"Nelson Mandela," Maybeck told Finn.

"You guys come with me," Finn instructed as he spotted Jez and the woman again. They were well down Main Street, heading toward the castle.

Amanda sat up suddenly, surprising them all. Willa yelped.

"Don't!" Amanda gasped, looking directly at Finn. "You have no idea . . . of their powers."

She slumped back, in that same lost state again.

"We've got to go. Now!" he told the boys.

The three boys hurried down Main Street.

"What about, you know . . . ?" Maybeck asked.

Finn tapped his chest. "I brought the pens."

"Aren't we going the wrong way? Shouldn't we be going to the fire station?"

"Don't ask me how, but Jez did this to Charlene and Amanda. Made them sick."

"That's ridiculous!" Maybeck said, his voice raspy. They were nearly running.

Finn explained, "Jez hooked up with a *witch!* In costume? Or for real? Super skinny. Long black hair. Sound like anyone we've seen lately? And oh, by the way, Jez just happens to be wearing long white gloves."

"Can I just say, you've completely lost it," Maybeck said. "And by completely, I mean one hundred percent."

"Gloves. Jez is wearing white gloves tonight. They

go to her elbow. Amanda and I saw those same gloves at—"

"The car wash," Maybeck answered. He'd seen them too.

Finn said, "Jez is a witch. And so's her mother." Philby and Maybeck looked stunned. "You want me to prove it, you'll come with me."

Following now, Philby said, "What if you happen to be right? In that case, what are we doing chasing a witch and her daughter? I mean, how stupid can we be?"

Maybeck huffed. "I'm going to have you guys institutionalized. Am I the only *sane* person left?"

"Wait!" Finn said, stopping them. They ducked behind a pillar in front of a Main Street shop. He pointed. Jez and the woman turned left at the plaza, just before the castle.

"How much do you want to bet they're heading to Pirates?"

Remembering the conversation on the monorail, Philby said, "Amanda told us Jez disappeared there."

"A figure of speech," Maybeck interjected. "That's all!"

As Finn led them left off the street as well, Maybeck said more seriously, "Listen, I've been there: where Charlene and Amanda are right now. Feeling sick like that. You do not want to mess with these people."

"They aren't people," Finn said. "That's the whole point. If they were people, then Wayne and the others could deal with them. This is up to us, you guys. No one else is going to do this."

"We're going in there after them?" Philby said. Jez and the woman arrived at the entrance to Pirates of the Caribbean. Sure enough, they headed inside.

"I do *not* like this," Maybeck said. "What happened to voting?"

"All in favor?" Finn asked. He and Philby raised their hands.

Maybeck groaned.

They stopped short of the entrance and stared warily at the old Spanish-style building.

"Okay," Philby said, "now I'm scared."

At night, in the midst of a Halloween costume party, Pirates of the Caribbean took on a more menacing feel, something each boy felt as he entered. Flamenco guitar music echoed from walls that flickered in the light of dim lanterns. And while the mood was festive, the Halloween party was a special event, so the crowds were much smaller than usual. The result was an attraction with deserted hallways and a hollow echo to every sound.

The boys hurried down a stone corridor. Finn had lost sight of Jez and her mother just as he heard the older woman's raspy voice saying, "Over here."

This was followed by a slight squeak of metal, a door swinging on hinges, and a resounding clang that reverberated off the walls.

"You hear that?" Maybeck asked.

The trio slowed. As they reached a sharp turn in the hall, Maybeck bent down, pretending to tie his running shoe, to let a group of eager teens race past them. When the hall was empty again, Philby pointed to a short staircase set into the wall, cordoned off by a chain.

To the right of the hall was a pit, a jail cell holding a pair of pirate figures engaged in a game of chess.

Maybeck hurried forward, jumped the chain, and climbed the short stairs. He reported back down to the others, "There's a pair of cannons and a kind of turret thing. Looks like the top of a fort or something."

Philby, ever the academic, explained, "It's a mock-up of a battlement, with twin eight-pound cannons and their shot in woven baskets." He'd done his homework, as usual.

Finn's attention remained on the jail cell and the sturdy iron bars mounted into the concrete. He tested its door, which swung open, making the same eerie squeak they'd heard only moments before.

Excited voices rang from the entrance to the attraction. More people coming.

Maybeck whispered softly, "If we're going in, we're going in. We can't stand around staring at it."

The boys stepped inside the heavy jail cell door and Finn pulled it shut.

They ducked into shadow as several groups of kids hurried past toward the start of the ride.

Finn then motioned down into the pit and the two pirates playing chess. It was a long way down, and there were no stairs.

Philby found a weighted rope connected to an

overhead pulley. "Care to take the elevator?" He tested the rope, held on tightly, and stepped off. He floated to the bottom of the pit. A moment later the other boys had reached the jail's floor.

"Okay, this is *really* weird," Finn said, "but I know this guy." He pointed to one of the pirates. He knew this figure from the laser battle. Looking more carefully, he realized that he recognized *both* pirates. He dared to reach over and gently poke the arm of the nearest pirate. Thankfully, it was a model, like a mannequin, and he relaxed.

They emerged into a long, straight hallway that lay in shadowy twilight. Jail cells lined both sides.

"It's a . . . prison," Maybeck said.

Finn stopped and examined a shiny piece of metal that hung from one of the doors. It turned out to be a padlock. A sparkling *new* padlock. Each of the cells was secured with a similar lock, all brand new. On further inspection, many of the hinges to the cell doors had been recently repaired. Fresh weld marks abounded.

"This has all been fixed up," Philby said. "And recently. What's with that?"

"Padlocks," Finn said. "A hundred padlocks stolen. Remember what Wayne said?" He recalled his father mentioning welding gear being stolen. The Overtakers.

Philby handled one of the padlocks. "You're not saying—"

"You want to explain it? Go ahead!" Finn said.

Maybeck said, "Listen, this makes sense. These cells are huge. Each cell could hold what, ten, maybe twenty people?"

The boys continued through the gloomy jail.

Philby did the math. "That means you could lock up *hundreds* of people down here. You realize that?"

Finn said, "Park employees."

"They're planning a takeover," Philby said. "They stole the locks. They fixed up the cells."

Finn stated, "They obviously plan to use these."

"This is exactly what Wayne is afraid of," Philby said. "Now I get it: if they organize, and if they have real powers, it's possible they could take over the park."

"And once they did," Finn said, "what would happen to the guests who arrived?"

"It's not just a jail, guys. Welcome to the dungeon." Maybeck pointed to a door at the end of the jails. The door hung open, revealing a tomblike darkness beyond. "And yes," he added quickly, "I realize how stupid this sounds."

Finn reminded, "Remember, we're not crossed over. We're not going to turn invisible. We're not going to glow. We're not going to walk through walls. So if we run, we run."

"I'm all over that," Maybeck said.

They paused at the door and listened to high-pitched voices faintly coming through the darkness.

Philby whispered, "I suggest we stick to the shadows."

"Shadows?" Maybeck questioned. "It's pitch-black in there."

"It won't be," Philby assured him.

Maybeck said, "No matter what, we hang together. You do *not* want to go one-on-one with these people."

"If they are people," Philby said, meaning it as a joke. No one laughed.

"Any advice?" Finn asked.

"Don't underestimate their power over you," Maybeck said. "You don't want to look into their eyes. I remember looking into a pair of eyes—the cold got much more intense."

"So . . . try to think of other things, or what?" Finn asked.

"Yeah. They definitely put thoughts into your head, which feel like your own ideas. But they aren't your ideas at all. They're like orders. We ought to go through that door with our minds already occupied," Maybeck suggested. "If we go through at all."

"Occupied with *what*?" Philby asked.

Maybeck answered, "What's the ugliest, weirdest monster you've ever seen? In a movie, in your imagination, in your sleep? Try that. And don't let go of it. Fight fire with fire." He added, "Jez is so nice, it's hard to see her as dangerous. That's when you start losing power, when the cold really gets going."

"And you couldn't have told us this before we decided to come here?" Philby asked, annoyed.

"I didn't remember any of this. Swear I didn't. Not until just now. But man, I'm telling you, it's all coming back in a big way."

"Are we all set?" Finn asked.

The boys nodded.

Finn led the way through the door, his feet feeling the way in front of him. The darkness gave way to a descending stone staircase. Partway down, the stairs turned left and a dim electric light shone overhead. More lights up ahead.

The stagnant, musty air grew quickly cool. The walls dripped and green slime ran down them like thick paint. The boys sloshed through several shallow puddles. Finn followed two sets of wet shoe prints now, from puddle to puddle.

All at once the space opened into a square room. The stone ceiling was supported by four enormous stone pillars, each with a different animal head carved onto it. The carvings were of ghoulish, evil faces, half animal, half human—hideous, with bug eyes and tongues sticking out. Stone benches ran along the walls. This was some kind of gathering place.

The air felt even colder now.

Finn counted three dark doorways leading from the room. Jez and the woman could have gone through any one of them.

Philby dropped to one knee, looking for wet prints to follow. He crawled forward on his hands and knees and ended facing the middle of the three doorways. He pointed silently.

Finn nodded.

The boys entered a dank, narrow tunnel with walls close enough to touch on both sides at the same time. It grew ever gloomier. There was barely any light. A suffocating staleness hung in the air.

Finn toed his way carefully ahead, encountering yet another short flight of stone steps. A single bare bulb lit the place where the tight passageway ended at a second, vast open space, a room carved from sandstone. A half dozen columns, all connected by carved arches, rose like tree trunks from the floor.

It reminded Finn of Escher's Keep. It was almost as if Escher himself had once been here. Many similar patterns and designs adorned the room. Had Walt Disney once shown this room to the great artist?

Maybeck crossed his arms tightly. "Temperature alert," he whispered. "Arctic air mass."

It was an unnatural cold. A far too familiar cold. They were drawing closer to the source.

Philby, in the lead, led them to the right. Noticing that the chill was reduced here, they reversed directions, following the cold like a bloodhound follows a scent.

A tremor of terror ran through Finn. What were they thinking in coming here? A spiral staircase that looked like a hermit crab's shell rose to his left. Another set of narrow stone steps descended straight ahead. This place was a labyrinth. But more strangely, it was also a forced-perspective hallway. The deeper they penetrated into the room, the lower the ceiling. The effect made the room appear much longer than it actually was.

Finn, no giant himself, ducked as the moist sandstone caught his hair. Spiderwebs stuck to his face. He clawed at them.

The boys heard hushed voices to their right. They changed direction, hunched, and stooped by the sloped ceiling.

"Valor is such a dangerous thing." The same voice from the teepee: Maleficent.

The boys stopped and turned in unison.

She stood alongside a column. She'd hidden behind it. They'd walked right past her. "Like bees to sugar water," she said.

She now blocked their return route.

She said, "If you didn't care so much about your two girlfriends up there, you wouldn't have followed us down here. And if you didn't follow us, then how would we ever get you to give us the pen?"

They'd been tricked. Jez and Maleficent had *wanted* to be followed.

Maybeck made a quick move to his left, but with a simple wave of her gloved hand Maleficent threw up a series of white vibrating lines that connected one column to the next. A cage of light. The lines hummed and sparked with electricity. They added light to the gloominess.

A second wave of her hands erected more lines, intricately connected. She had created a complex fence around the boys.

She said, "You're familiar with shock collars for dogs? Wireless fences? Same concept. I don't advise testing it, but be my guests, if you must."

The light allowed Finn to see the purple of her robes. Too scared to talk, he summoned his courage, refusing to look directly at her while at the same time keeping a monstrous image in his mind's eye.

"We know you have it on you," she said, "you clever child. Now . . . place the pen down on the floor there. As soon as you do, your girlfriends will feel fine."

Silence. Not even Maybeck responded with his usual sarcasm.

Philby's eyes danced toward the sparking white lines that caged them. Finn could feel him plotting escape.

Finn felt it worth a lie. "It might help if I knew what you were talking about."

"You insolent young man."

"We were there. One Man's Dream." Jez stepped out from behind another column.

"One Witch's Dream, too," Maleficent said. "These parks grow so . . . claustrophobic—don't you think?"

Seeing these two side by side, Finn realized how different they looked. It was hard to believe Jez was this woman's daughter. And now he felt awful for doubting Amanda. Now she sat semiconscious somewhere above them.

"You two can go," Maleficent said to Philby and Maybeck. She swept her hand to one side and the fence sputtered and vanished. *"Omnia haec obliviscantur!"* she chanted musically, then said, "When you reach the surface, you will remember none of what has gone on here. Neither the events nor the way down. All you will recall is going to the restroom together. You don't know where Finn is. Haven't seen him in a while. Now go."

The two boys remained rooted firmly in place. "No way!" Philby said.

"Silly, silly boy." She clapped her gloved hands together. Philby seemed to lose every bone in his body. He fell to the floor in a heap of unwilling limbs and muscle, a lump of flesh.

"I'm giving you a very generous opportunity here. Terry knows better than to disobey, don't you, Terry?"

Maybeck's lips moved, but no sound came out.

"I can add some pain, if you like," she said to Philby.

"No!" Maybeck said, reaching for Philby.

"Go!" Finn instructed them.

They looked pained to hear this from him.

"Go," he repeated.

Losing her patience, Maleficent asked, "Or do you prefer fire?"

Her left hand suddenly held a ball of flame. She blew it out.

"Or wind?" The room swirled with a gale force that blew dust into their eyes and knocked the boys off their feet. Neither Jez's robes nor her mother's so much as fluttered.

"Want to play some more?" she asked.

Maleficent lit another ball of flame in her hand. She blew on it, sending it rolling directly for Maybeck. It exploded in a puff of black smoke just before reaching him.

Helping Philby up, Finn leaned in and whispered, "Keep an image in your head. Focus on something. Protect your memory." He gave him a little shove. "Now, go!" he said more loudly.

Maybeck led Philby by the arm. They hurried out of the room.

When they were gone, Finn said to the witch, "You're head of the Overtakers."

She cackled an edgy laugh. "Me? Head? False compliments will get you nowhere with me, young man. I am but a humble servant to she who lives within. My powers are so small and insignificant. Do not waste your breath. I'm an errand runner, that's all."

Finn felt his knees go weak. There was something more powerful than she was?

She instructed him: "Now, put it on the floor. Do so, or suffer. Your choice."

"Make me," Finn said.

Maleficent waved her right hand and Finn's cape blew open. The assortment of pens and pencils taken from Walt's desk stuck out from the cape's inside pocket. The witch turned away and the cape fell shut.

"If you could make me hand it over, you would have," he told her. "But you can't. For some reason, you need me to cooperate. Why is that?"

He flashed open the cape again. And again, she averted her gaze.

"He protected against this, didn't he? Walt Disney," Finn said as he concealed the pens and pencils again.

Maleficent dared to venture a look at the pens, her eyes sparkling, as if Finn were holding a million dollars in gold.

He took hold of the pens and held them out toward her. Maleficent cowered away from him.

"Interesting," Finn said. "You need one of these pens or pencils, don't you? But which one?" He stepped forward. She moved back, and away, ducking behind the nearest column. "The real quill can *hurt* you, can't it? Dull your powers?" He understood then. This was how Wayne could stop the Overtakers.

"It can stop your plans, this pen, can't it? You need to get rid of it. Destroy it. Even just its existence has threatened you all these years."

"What do you know? You're just a boy! And we all know little boys shouldn't play with fire." With that, she pretended she was bowling. A large ball of fire rolled from her hand and across the floor at Finn. He dodged it easily enough, but then came a second, and a third.

Jez "caught" the balls of fire on the opposite side and bowled them back toward Maleficent. Finn, trapped in the middle, danced to avoid the flames.

A ball singed his cape. He couldn't keep this up for long. He found himself hopping around like an Irish step dancer.

"You will do exactly as I say," Maleficent instructed him, still bowling her fireballs at him.

Finn understood what he had to do. Dodging the fire as he landed, he scattered several of the pens across the stone floor. A ball of fire tumbled toward the pens.

"No!" the witch shouted. With a wave of her hand, the flaming balls vanished into wisps of black smoke and the tangy smell that follows a lightning storm.

So, Finn thought, she doesn't want to destroy the pen, and she can't touch it herself. She has a use for it, but is also afraid of its power.

"You think yourself so clever?" she called out angrily. She walked right through his electric cage, straight for the pens.

Finn dove across the floor, swept them up into his hand, and sprinted for the white sparking fence. She had passed through without so much as a spark.

When he was crossed over, Finn had been able to

walk through walls and counter the currents of Splash Mountain by concentrating on the DHI essence of his crossed-over body. So why not pass through this electric fence unharmed?

He focused on the single idea: I am light. I am nothing but light. Nothing can stop me if I'm nothing but light. Nothing can harm me if I'm—

Wham!

Reaching the fence at full stride, he was knocked back off his feet and onto the floor. He felt as if he'd been stabbed in the chest.

Maleficent seemed to float, not walk, as she approached. She towered over him. Scowling, the witch raised her arm, about to deliver a spell. Finn clutched the pens and jumped toward her, lightning fast. He thrust the pens in her face. Sparks flew as the pens connected with Maleficent. She flew back and fell to the stone floor.

"Your Grace?" Jez called out.

The witch lay on the stone floor, stunned. The electric fence sputtered.

Finn stepped closer to the fallen witch, the pens held in front of him like a sword. She recoiled, expecting him to strike again.

"Lower the fence!" he instructed Jez. He never took his eyes off Maleficent. She seemed to be gaining her strength back. "Lower the fence, or I'll do it again," Finn warned.

The bars of buzzing white lines sparked twice more and then vanished.

"Release Amanda and Charlene," he told her. When Jez hesitated, he stepped closer to Maleficent. The feeling of cold increased. Her strength was indeed returning. He needed Jez to do this quickly, before her mother came to her senses.

He stabbed at Maleficent with the fistful of pens. A second burst of sparks threw her down again.

"Okay!" Jez exclaimed. She waved her hands. "It's done."

Finn backed up and reached the stairway.

A weakened Maleficent lifted her head and said, "We will meet again, young man. We have unfinished business, you and I."

Finn turned and ran.

The kids needed the plans that had been stolen from Finn at One Man's Dream, and no one had any doubts as to who had taken them. Maleficent would return for the pen—the Stonecutter's Quill—with a vengeance. Whatever powers the pen and the plans possessed when combined, each side had their reasons for wanting what the other now possessed.

Before he left Mickey's Not-So-Scary Halloween Party, Finn paid Wayne a visit to explain the night's events.

"It's always such a noisy night," Wayne complained. He looked silly dressed in a pair of pajamas and a plaid robe. He wore Mickey and Minnie Mouse fuzzy slippers.

"We need your help."

"So it would seem. So it would seem." Wayne paced his small apartment over the fire station, glancing out the windows occasionally. Finn heard him mutter, "When will they go home?" Then he paced some more. "Two birds with one stone," he said, now addressing Finn.

"How's that?" Finn asked, impatient to hook back up with his friends and leave the park.

"I can help you—will help you—but it won't come without additional risk to us all. She has to be desperate to be bowling fire at your feet. Revealing herself like that." He studied the pens spread out on the small dining table, where Finn had put them. "You'll keep all of these, because they've obviously come in handy. Tomorrow's the day. They'll be expecting you by night, of course, because that's when you're usually here. So it can't be night. It must be day. Furthermore, if you're to secure the plans, then you must be a boy, not crossed over."

"But we can touch and hold things when we're crossed over. I can get those plans back."

"You can't do that where I'm sending you," Wayne countered. "You'll have to be yourself. The others as well. And you'll need disguises, or you'll get caught." Wayne paused, thinking hard. "Cast-member costumes, you understand? Employees. Each of you. I can help there as well."

"But why? Where are you sending us?"

"You showed me," Wayne said. "I might have never figured this out by myself."

"Showed you what?"

"Where's the one place that a weakened Maleficent can hide without being questioned?"

"Here in the park."

"I mean, *where* in the park?"

"Whatever ride, whatever attraction she's part of."

"But that's the point. She isn't part of one," Wayne answered. "Her role is over at the studios. She's in Fantasmics. That's all she does here—that one show. She turns herself into the dragon. Maybe in real life as well."

"I don't understand."

"I'm an old man talking to himself, that's all. Back to the important question: where can she hide in the Magic Kingdom?"

"Out in the open?" Finn guessed.

"Precisely. And if I were her, if I'd stolen these plans and then led boys down to my secret lair, I would need someplace new to lay low. The boys might tell people about the dungeons. They could be searched. I could be caught. I need a place no one can find me."

"But where?" Finn asked, feeling as if they were talking in circles.

"We'll need all five of you to dress as cast members. You'll meet me at the Transportation and Ticket Center, bus stop number five, at nine o'clock tomorrow morning. Can you make that?"

"Tomorrow's Sunday. Probably. I suppose so."

"Make sure you do," he advised.

"What did you mean by 'two birds with one stone'?"

"We're going to use her own tactics against her. If you manage to get the plans, she'll come after you. She'll want to stop you from getting them to me, especially now that she knows you have the pen."

"So?"

"You're going to lead her into a trap." His old eyes brightened.

"You're going to use us as bait?"

Wayne looked at Finn. His features softened. "How terribly impolite of me. It has been so long, you see. We're so close now. So very close." He straightened up and looked Finn in the eye. "I need your help—yours and the others'—in catching Maleficent. It is a task not without risk, but one I assure you well worth the effort, if you're game. This is, I believe, what Walt had intended all along—the capture of an Overtaker, the beginning of the end for them." He paused and allowed Finn to think through his proposal. Then he asked, "So? Will you help me?"

At nine the next morning, Finn stood with the others in line at bus stop number five at the Transportation and Ticket Center.

A large bus pulled up. The door swung open, and

from behind the wheel Wayne motioned them inside. "Well?" the old guy said, "Hurry it up!"

The kids piled on, and Wayne shut the door and drove off. They were all alone in the otherwise empty bus.

"There isn't time," Wayne said. "There's a bag for each of you."

Finn's name was written on one of five grocery bags. Inside was a costume.

"Put it on," Wayne instructed. "Ladies to the back."

Some blankets had been strung across the rear seats to provide the girls privacy.

"Gentlemen up front."

Wayne turned the bus at the next corner, and the boys, all in various degrees of undress, had to hold on to keep their balance.

Wayne picked up the microphone and announced so the girls could hear as well, "I'll bring you in around the back of the park at Frontierland. You'll enter the tunnels from there."

"Tunnels?" Finn asked.

"After that, it's up to the five of you, I'm afraid."

When the boys were dressed, Charlene and Willa came forward. Willa wore an old-fashioned blue-striped dress and a puffy-sleeved blouse printed with pastel flowers, the uniform of food-service workers in

Frontierland. Charlene wore a skirt and top of a deck-hand on the paddle wheel steamboat that circled Tom Sawyer Island.

"Listen, all of you! There's a schedule in place we must keep to in order for this to work."

Wayne was one of the worst drivers Finn had ever met. The bus nearly sideswiped two cars, then veered left and scraped its wheels against the curb, before smashing back down to the roadway.

"Okay, we're listening," Finn said, realizing that the old goat was agitated.

Philby was dressed as a boatman on the Jungle Cruise. Finn was a newspaper boy from Main Street. Maybeck wore a turban-topped outfit from the Magic Carpets of Aladdin.

Wayne pulled the bus over and threw open the door. Amanda boarded.

"She is necessary to our plans," Wayne announced.

Amanda looked Finn in the eye and then, without saying anything, took a seat in the middle of the bus.

Wayne explained, "Amanda has the run of the place. She's not on the DHI watch list. She'll act as sentry and guide when you need her."

Now inside the Magic Kingdom, Wayne slowed the bus next to a large white building that, according to its sign, had something to do with waste disposal. A wide metal tube, connected to the building, extended out from an earthen bank. A paved road led up the rise to a very large double gate in the wooden wall. Flowers and shrubs covered a small hill that bordered a tall wooden fence, which was behind Frontierland.

Wayne spun to face them, still behind the wheel. He nervously checked his wristwatch. "You'll wear these ID tags around your necks at all times. But turn them so they face in, so the ID picture doesn't show." Wayne had borrowed some ID tags for them.

"What's this building?" Maybeck asked. Dressed as Ali Baba, or whoever he was, Finn thought he looked pretty cool.

Wayne answered. "This is important to you, Finn. Have you ever seen a garbage bag being carried around inside the park?" Wayne asked.

All five shook their heads.

"This building is why. All the park's trash travels underground through a series of steel tubes. Those tubes terminate here, where the trash is compacted, and then shipped off to a dump. The process is automated. I've briefed Amanda."

She remained in the back, silent and studious. Briefed Amanda about the trash? Finn wondered. He kept his mouth shut.

"Once I get you inside," Wayne instructed, "you're

on your own. The Utilidor here—that's what the park tunnels are called—is complicated and big. The corridors are more like underground roads than sidewalks. There are golf carts and electric buggies down there, so keep alert and don't get hit. Cast members know the Utilidor well, and you're cast members now. You'll need to look comfortable."

"What about Maleficent?" Finn asked. "The plans?"

"Terrence," Wayne said to Maybeck, "what's likely the coldest room in an office building?"

"The computer room," Maybeck answered. "The server center."

"So where's the safest, most comfortable place for someone who likes the cold to spend time?"

"A refrigerator?" Charlene answered, not paying enough attention.

"One possibility, yes, and one that you and Willa will pursue. There's an entire section of the Utilidor devoted to cold food storage."

"The computer center," Maybeck said, answering Wayne's question.

"The servers are housed at the back of what we call the Control Room. That's for you and the boys." Wayne warned them, "Stay alert for a sudden drop in temperature. That's what you're looking for. The missing plans won't be far away. We need those plans." Wayne looked troubled and concerned. "The point is, from what Finn described, he wounded Maleficent. Weakened her. He also made it impossible for her to remain below Pirates of the Caribbean. I believe she's taken to the Utilidor, where, looking like a cast member, no one would question or detain her. Your job is to get those plans from her and to flush her out. To draw her out. We will handle the rest."

"We?" Philby asked.

"You leave that to me, young man." He looked between all six kids, for now Amanda was standing just behind Finn. "Are you ready?"

A moment of hesitation settled over the kids. Then, one by one, they nodded. Even Charlene.

Wayne's face brightened again. "Once you've got the plans and you're topside," he said, "that's when the chase begins. I'm afraid you may literally need to run for your lives. Maleficent is not likely to be a good loser. Finn takes the plans. Amanda will guide him back here." Again, Wayne took a moment to make eye contact with each of the kids. He ended with Finn. "You'll do *exactly* as she says."

Finn glanced back at Amanda.

He didn't feel good about this. She revealed nothing of what she might be thinking.

Finn felt there was an unusually strong bond

between Wayne and Amanda. Were they related some-how? Without question, Finn thought, Amanda was no ordinary girl.

Wayne threw the bus door open, and the kids hurried out.

Inside the Magic Kingdom, the sun shone brightly. Finn's costume warmed up. He thought the air smelled like Thanksgiving. It took him a minute to spot the turkey leg being gnawed on by a big man wearing a Hard Rock Café shirt.

The six kids and Wayne passed into the park through a high wooden fence, with Thunder Mountain to their right. Past the ride and through another door marked for cast members, they entered a room with dull green walls. They saw an elevator door, scratched and in need of paint, with a single arrow pointing down. A large sign bolted to the cinderblock wall above the adjacent set of descending stairs cautioned: CAST MEMBERS ONLY PLEASE.

"I'll go first," Wayne announced. "Girls, you'll follow me to food service. Terrence, you know what you're looking for. Good luck, everyone."

Finn felt his throat catch. There was only one reason Wayne could be doing this so soon on the heels of the previous night.

It isn't safe.

They had to accomplish this before Maleficent

regained all her powers. Though Finn wondered what would become of them if she already had.

Wayne's white head bobbed down the stairs, followed closely by Charlene and then Willa. The boys heard a heavy door open and close. Then silence. Finn's throat was bone-dry. His palms were sweating.

Maybeck went first. He descended the stairs, suddenly consumed by shadow. Again, the sound of the door opening and falling shut.

That door swallowed his friends. He hoped he'd see them again.

Philby went next.

Finn then worked his way down and, hand on the door, reminded himself to stay calm. He tugged on the door and opened it to a strange, unfamiliar world. They found themselves in a tunnel that ran a great distance in both directions. People in Disney costumes walked in groups while battery-operated vehicles plied the corridors.

The Utilidor was physically much wider, much bigger—enormous, really!—than Finn had imagined it would be: an underground road of sorts with doors leading from it.

Actors dressed as nonhuman animated Disney characters, like Mickey and Minnie and Donald Duck, paraded past, each wearing or carrying a mask large enough to cover their whole head. There were others dressed as human characters, wearing makeup but without masks—Belle and Snow White, Peter Pan, and Mulan. The walkarounds, they were called.

A small electric truck zoomed past, stacked high with cans of soda and bottled water. Finn looked to see Charlene and Willa headed in the same direction the truck was going.

He followed a short distance behind Philby, who in turn followed Maybeck. The boys were now moving in the opposite direction from the girls.

Overhead, along the tunnel's ceiling, thick cables and pipes hung. No Disney music played down here. Instead the boys heard only the whine of the vehicles, the steady *whoosh* of piped-in air, and the gentle murmur of voices.

Finn passed a girl with Cinderella's hair and face. But she wore blue jeans and a tank top, not yet in costume.

The boys walked briskly for well over five minutes before finally coming to another tunnel. Maybeck followed the signs as Wayne had told him. This new tunnel gradually sloped downward, leveled out, and ran another fifty yards before climbing again, then it dead-ended at yet another busy tunnel. Finn followed to the right, Philby and Maybeck just ahead.

Offices and unidentified rooms lined the route. It

was extremely busy down here, with people coming and going like worker bees. Finn caught a glimpse of a cafeteria. He passed signs for the PROPERTY ROOM, a barber shop, and a women's hair salon. *A city!* The tunnel veered left.

Philby and Maybeck slowed and pretended to read from a bulletin board.

"It's just up ahead," Maybeck said in a low voice. "The timing is critical because there's a coffee break coming up. Wayne thinks our best shot at getting in there is during the coffee break."

Finn took a sip from a water fountain, stealing a look down the hall. They waited. A few minutes later three workers—two men and a woman—left the door marked CONTROL ROOM.

The boys approached the door and entered.

Inside they faced row after row of steel shelving, like bookshelves in a library, floor to ceiling. Instead of books, the shelves were filled with thousands of tiny blinking lights, red, yellow and orange: rack-mounted computers.

It was chilly in here.

Maybeck hurried down the second-to-last row, saying softly, "Wayne's point is that no one will notice Maleficent's cold aura in a cold place like this. He said the servers are in a back room."

Sure enough, they soon stood facing several steel doors, all unmarked.

Finn stepped forward and touched the back of his hand to each door in succession. The middle door was noticeably colder.

Finn wondered for how many years—how many decades—Maleficent had been confined to the various tunnels and lairs beneath the Magic Kingdom. It seemed no wonder she'd turned to the dark side of her powers.

"How do we do this?" Maybeck asked, now that he'd led them here.

"I don't think we knock," Philby said.

"Actually . . . maybe we do," Finn said, surprising the other two. He thought for a minute and said, "Have either of you ever run track?"

Maybeck nodded.

"How about the relay?" Finn asked.

Maybeck nodded again.

"Drivers, start your engines," Finn said. He pulled the boys into a three-way huddle and told them his plan.

"Knock, knock!" Finn said loudly. "It's your favorite Disney Host Interactive," he announced. He kept one eye on the wall clock. The coffee break was scheduled to last fifteen minutes. Six of those minutes were behind them.

No answer. Seven minutes gone; eight minutes remaining.

"I've come to offer you a deal."

Spines of ice crept up the edges of the closed door. Finn could picture the witch standing just on the other side. His knees felt weak, but he had to go through with this.

He raised his voice. "We're through. We're done. Wayne—he's an old guy who sent us here to steal something from you—but we've had a change of heart. We want to destroy the server. The computer that generates our DHIs. We don't want to do this anymore." Still nothing, though the ice on the door thickened. "We don't know which server it is. We don't know what to do. You help us—*without* hurting us—and we'll give you the pens."

The doorknob went white with frost. She was holding it from the other side.

"You're thinking this is a trap," Finn said. "And you're right to think that. But it isn't. We just want to go home. We want to sleep at night. Please . . . help us, and you'll have what you want."

The doorknob turned.

Maleficent stood in the doorway. She had not fully recovered from Finn's zapping her the night before. She looked older, slightly yellow in the cheeks. Behind her, on a stack of more computers, Finn saw the scroll of plans she had stolen from him at One Man's Dream.

Finn and Maybeck backed up a step. Philby was nowhere to be seen.

"Which server?" Finn asked.

"And we need whatever back-up server they have, as well," Maybeck said. "Once we're gone, we don't want them able to bring us back."

Maleficent glared at them with her eyelids lowered menacingly. She was either half dead or ready to kill.

"I'm sorry for what I did," Finn said. "I didn't know." Finn realized he'd zapped a good deal of the power from her. He'd drained her. She was like a battery running out of juice.

She said nothing, just stood there blinking, looking devilish. She gathered her strength and said, "Jez likes you, or I would have hurt you last night when I had the chance."

"That's comforting to know," Finn said. "I'll put down the pens. You can have it. But first you'll show us the right server."

"First the pens," she said. "You think I'd trust you like that?"

"And why should I trust you?"

"This is your idea, not mine. Besides, once I have the pen, what threat are you?"

Finn concealed his smirk as he shrugged. "Have it your way," he said.

He withdrew the group of pens and pencils from his pocket and placed them on the ground.

Maleficent approached them like a kid nearing a Christmas tree. She seemed to have more energy. Her eyes flared open in expectation.

Finn took several more steps backward, Maybeck right next to him.

But behind Maleficent, the door to the back room swung slowly away from the wall, and there stood Philby. In his right hand Philby clutched a fistful of pens and pencils tightly.

Maleficent bent toward the pens on the floor, clearly cautious. But as she drew closer she saw modern brand names on the pens. She looked up through fiery eyes.

"Now!" Finn shouted.

Philby charged from behind and did just as Finn had told him: holding the pens extended, he drove his fist into the witch.

At that same moment, she turned around.

A blinding flash erupted as the pens made contact. Maleficent rose from the floor and was thrown violently past Finn and Maybeck and into the heavy black shelves.

Maybeck sprinted forward into the back room, grabbed the roll of plans, and headed for the main door.

Philby, stunned by what he'd done, passed the pens to Finn, leaving behind on the floor the pens the boys had collected from a desk at the front of the control room.

Philby was next out the door.

"What's going on here?" A big man blocked Finn's exit.

Just then a shower of sparks and spurts of flame rose from where Maleficent lay pinned to the computer shelves, impaled onto a stack of electrical outlets and surge suppressors. As the electricity flowed through her body, beneath the smoke and spitting sparks, Finn saw her skin color return to a rich green. The electricity fed her.

"What—is—that—?" asked the office manager.

Maleficent's bloodshot eyes flashed open and locked onto Finn. He'd never seen eyes so angry, so mean and vicious. So powerful. And they were aimed at him. Only at him.

The office manager staggered toward a fire extinguisher hanging from the wall.

Finn made for the door.

Maleficent pulled herself loose from the metal shelving as a shower of sparks cascaded overhead and cried, "Aaaah! I needed that!"

She flew out the door. Literally.

The office manager fainted.

F inn hit the tunnel running. Behind him raced a blur of green and black as Maleficent sped through the air, her arm pointing in front of her and leading the way.

Closing the distance.

The boys ran side by side now, Maleficent behind them, and closing fast. Like a shell game, the boys passed the plans back and forth between them, then switched positions as they ran and passed the plans again. For someone behind them, where Maleficent now followed, it grew impossible to determine which boy had the plans.

Then, just as Maleficent was nearly upon them, the boys split up, running in three different directions.

Maybeck mumbled, perhaps a little too loudly for his own good, "I've got them! Don't worry. *Just run!*"

Finn took an exit door to his left. He raced up the stairs at a furious speed, glancing behind. No Maleficent. She'd followed Maybeck.

Finn broke into blinding daylight. He checked the tube of papers tucked into his waist, thrilled the plan had worked. Fresh air. Park music. For a moment Finn couldn't figure out where he was. A cast member door led out into Tomorrowland. That was wrong! He was out of position. Finn fled through the door and out onto a busy concourse.

At midday, the area bustled with activity, a steady stream of guests in a chaotic mass of T-shirts, shorts, and the sweet smell of suntan lotion.

How long would it take for Maleficent to discover their trickery?

The plan had been to rendezvous with Amanda on the bridge between Tomorrowland and the Central Plaza. But which way? Finn had left the Utilidor via the wrong exit.

He heard the crowd scream to his right. He was familiar with all sorts of sounds in the Magic Kingdom, but this particular roar sounded out of place.

A second later, Maybeck came out of the same CAST MEMBERS ONLY door. He was out of breath and sweating.

"She's after Philby," he told Finn.

Another scream broke from the distance.

Some little kids shouted, "Aladdin! Aladdin!" and cut through the thick crowds to reach Maybeck, who they mistook for the character. Maybeck tried to get away from them. Parents called after their kids to be polite. A line formed behind Maybeck as he and Finn set out walking.

Maybeck said under his breath, "We should have lost the wardrobe."

"I don't know," Finn said, "maybe we can use this."

He handed Maybeck one of the pens.

"You're kidding me!"

The children caught up and surrounded them both, their autograph notebooks out and ready.

"Sign some autographs, *Aladdin*," Finn said encouragingly.

With clenched teeth, Maybeck asked in a whisper, "How do you spell *Aladdin*?"

Finn spelled it for him as yet another excited scream pealed from the crowd—this time much closer. A sea of park guests parted to his right. A green witch. Maleficent. She walked quickly and deliberately and was just scary enough looking to hold her admirers at bay.

"Head down!" Finn called out.

Maybeck ducked, continuing to scribble out autographs furiously.

The green-faced witch and her following sea of fans passed them by.

Finn backed away from the clot of eager children.

"That's all!" Finn said, though to little effect.

Maybeck was suddenly hooked on this autograph writing. He made no attempt to stop.

"Aladdin!" Philby called out. "You're going to *be late!*"

Maybeck finally gave it up. He made his apologies, and he and Finn moved on.

The crowd up ahead, the group following Maleficent, stopped, colliding into one another. This, because the witch had stopped and turned. But why?

Finn moved in the other direction. He came face-to-face with Jez.

"Give us the pen and the plans, and we won't hurt you," she said.

Several things happened at once. First, Finn spotted a group of four or five seagulls clustered atop a high white fence. Then he saw Amanda. She stood inside the same white fence, the gulls perched overhead. She signaled Finn to join her. Third, Jez reached for the plans—and stole them from him.

"Go!" Finn ordered Maybeck. And there was Philby standing next to Amanda, also beckoning them over to the fence.

Finn dove at Jez, knocked her down, and took the plans back. She sat up on the pavement, mumbled something, and cast a spell at Finn.

He felt a sharp pain flood through him. His knees went weak. That dreaded sense of cold overcame him.

Jez smiled at her success, got to her feet, and stepped toward him. Finn fought against the spell by thinking of himself as pure light—as a DHI—even though he was just Finn Whitman, the boy. He allowed her no power over him, refused to give into her. As he did, something strange happened. His fingers tingled.

A woman in the crowd gasped, "Oh, my gosh! Look who it is!"

Finn was crossing over—becoming his DHI.

He mentally pushed against Jez. The harder he pushed, the more of his body turned to light—a hologram.

The next spell she tried to cast passed right through him and turned a small tree just behind him to solid ice.

The crowd applauded and cheered, children shouting, "More! More!"

Jez lunged at Finn but she, too, passed right through him.

Again, the crowd cheered.

She dared to try again. This time, Finn stepped into her and stopped. He moved with her in perfect lock-step, able somehow to know her every thought.

She spun in circles, trying to rid herself of him. They were a single entity now: spinning and glowing. Two kids in one. The crowd went wild.

Finn resisted the cold. He felt warmth replace it.

He heard her calling out, "Your Grace!" She sounded desperate and afraid.

The crowd roared their approval; a spinning vortex of light, and the girl's wild cries for help.

Finn stepped away from her, and Jez spun to a stop, dazed. She raised her head slowly while studying her hands, her arms, touching her forearms as if they didn't belong to her.

"I can't believe it." As her eyes met Finn's, she cried out, "I'm . . . free!"

Free from what? Finn wondered.

"You did it!" Jez said to Finn, her eyes bright, her voice excited. "No more cold. No more Maleficent. You freed me!"

With that, the most startling thing happened. Jez changed, she transformed, before Finn's eyes. The crowd applauded as her hair changed color, from jet-black to a sandy blond. Her eyebrows and eyelashes became lighter as well, and a few freckles appeared on her cheeks. She was, without question, a different girl, a beautiful girl, and yet . . . familiar. Finn couldn't get over the feeling that he'd met her before, that he knew her, this new girl. And then, as he glanced back to his friends and saw Amanda there calling for him, a spike of astonishment filled him, and he felt the DHI dissolve and the real Finn return. Amanda's face filled with light, with an expression of joy Finn had never seen. Tears filled her eyes.

Finn looked back and forth between the two girls, Jez and Amanda, and—

It couldn't be. . . .

But it was.

They were sisters, twins perhaps, not identical, but close to it.

Only then did he understand Amanda's efforts, her never giving up. Only then did he come to wonder if Amanda wasn't some kind of witch herself—a good witch.

The crowd exploded into celebration.

Maleficent's green form streaked toward them.

As Finn—a boy again—reached the fence, he faced Amanda. "Why didn't you tell me?"

"You weren't ready," she said.

Amanda stood in front of a large yellow cylinder sticking out of the ground, with a thick, circular, steel trapdoor on top. A number of warning posters instructed proper use.

"The others went ahead," Amanda said. "Go!"

Finn looked down. "But it's a trash chute."

"Go! Feet first." She opened it. "Quickly! Jump!" She seemed distracted.

Finn followed her line of sight. Maleficent had

caught up to Jez. But Jez held her hands in front of her, and try as Maleficent might, she could not get close to the girl. Raging with anger, Maleficent suddenly saw Finn.

Finn asked Amanda, "Is Jez who I think she is?"

"Jess, not Jez, not any more. How can we ever thank you?" The tears spilled from her eyes. "We couldn't break the spell ourselves."

"Then she is— Then you are—" Finn's head swam.

But he stopped himself as Maleficent raised her hand to cast a spell.

Seeing this, Finn jumped down the trash chute.

From high overhead he heard Amanda's gleeful voice echo as he fell. "I'll never forget what you did!"

As he was sucked down the foul-smelling tube, Finn tucked the roll of plans away under his belt. He took a deep breath and gagged. He thought he might throw up.

The tube reeked of rotting trash. Gooey bits and sticky globs of rancid food and soggy litter stuck to him like leeches, licked his face and slopped into his hair and clothing. Again, he felt himself gag.

In the distance, far down the tube, echoing through the metal, Finn heard hoots and hollers—Maybeck and Philby.

The suction spit trash into his face. He slammed into some kind of mesh gate, an intersection of converging trash-evacuation tubes. On the other side, black garbage bags and trash raced past. Then the gate opened and it was his turn. He tumbled down and rolled into the next tube, picked up speed, and headed off again, upside down and backward.

Wind roared all around him. A garbage bag smashed into him. It broke open, its trash freed. Awful stuff raced around him and stuck to him. He braced himself just in time for another intersection. But this gate was open and he moved into a third, larger tube.

Aluminum cans peppered his head. Cellophane and cotton candy stuck to him. Diapers, orange peels, sticky popsicle sticks. He somersaulted to avoid this stuff, and there, behind him, came a dull green light. It grew ever larger. It moved quickly.

He was thrown into a back somersault. As he came around, he found himself facing Maleficent. Arms at her side, head forward, legs outstretched behind her, she flew effortlessly through the garbage tube, apparently unaffected by the suction.

"Miss me?" she wheezed.

She lunged. Her ice-cold hand grabbed for the scroll. Finn kicked out and pushed her back.

Her wide eyes narrowed in hatred. She lunged again.

Finn straightened himself out and gained speed. He briefly pulled away from her.

Through the roar, he heard her mumble: *"Anima transformatur!"* Finn ducked as she flicked her wrist at him. A sandwich bag next to him melted and re-formed into a rat. That spell had been meant for him. At once, the rat came alive, its tail swiping, its little feet clawing for purchase.

Maleficent closed the gap. Finn tore a hole in a garbage bag, scattering its contents.

He heard a clank of metal not far ahead: yet another gate.

The rat scrambled and scratched at Finn. If he and Maleficent crashed into a gate together, she would have him and the plans. He felt certain of it.

She wound up to deliver yet another spell, the two of them racing through the slimy tube. Finn grabbed hold of the clawing rat and threw it at her. Maleficent fought off the rat and came right for Finn.

He saw a small white circle grow larger and wider. The end of the tunnel! Finn could smell fresh air.

Trying to buy himself time, he shouted at her, "You forgot something: evil never wins in the Magic Kingdom."

She called back, "That depends on whose magic it is."

Propelled out the end of the trash tube, Finn flew

through the air and crashed into a sea of trash bags in an enormous steel collection box, like a railroad car. He scrambled toward the edge, where he saw Wayne and others, men and women, surrounding the huge collection bin.

"Hurry!" Wayne shouted.

Finn reached for the edge, pulled himself up and over, and fell to the ground, splatting, soaking wet with trash.

There he saw Philby and Maybeck, also covered in goo.

He watched as Maleficent shot out the end of the trash tube and into the giant container.

The team of adults quickly produced a net, dragging it from one end to the other and trapping her inside.

"To the bus! Quickly!" Wayne hollered, moving in that direction himself.

The other adults worked furiously to secure the net.

As Finn ran, he heard Maleficent's wails of complaint from the bin.

Maybeck, Philby, and Finn caught up to Wayne—the old guy limping along.

Finn shouted, "You're not going to—"

"No!" Wayne replied. "We don't kill anything here. Not even witches. We'll give her a taste of her own jail—the one you found—for a while. It'll give us time to determine how much power the Overtakers have gained. You've done well! We're almost through."

"Almost?" shouted all three boys, coming to a stop at once.

They all boarded the bus.

Finn handed him the plans and the pens.

Wayne looked back gratefully and said, "Good job, kids."

34

Looking out the window of the castle apartment, having crossed over just before ten o'clock, Finn thought the park looked beautiful.

He wondered if he'd ever know the truth about Amanda, if he'd ever see her again, for she'd been noticeably absent from school that Monday. He thought about Maleficent saying that there were Overtakers far more powerful than she was, and he wondered if more adventures lay in store for him and his new friends.

Willa was the last to cross over. She appeared in the room, wearing a cotton nightgown that flowed to her ankles. To explain this she said, "My mom put me to bed. Nothing much I could do about it."

Finn looked around at each of his new friends. He liked them all, though each for a different reason. He unrolled the faded blueprints of the park.

They examined them, fascinated to see how the park had started out. Wayne explained what they were looking at.

From the group of pens and pencils on the coffee

table, Wayne selected a boring-looking black one. It was fat and bulged. A very old fountain pen.

Wayne put on a pair of sunglasses. He passed out sunglasses to all the kids too, and told them to put them on as well.

"Now," Wayne said, "we finally put the two together."

"How will we know if it's right?" Finn asked.

Wayne's aged face twisted into a smile. "Believe me, we'll know."

Wayne contemplated the pen, then passed it to Finn, "This is for you, I think." He indicated a small metal lever on the end of the pen.

Finn picked up the pen, carefully unscrewed the cap, and hooked the small lever with his fingernail. He looked up at each of the others, their expectant eyes filled with curiosity and excitement.

"Hold it up high," Wayne instructed.

Finn did so, and pulled on the lever. A single drop of dark ink splashed down onto the plans. Finn, Wayne, and all the kids jumped back.

The drop of ink settled, then expanded and bled out into each and every faded line drawn onto the plans. It raced from one to another, spreading faster and faster. Faint lines became solid and bold.

The detailed plans transformed, one page after another. Some of what Finn saw was familiar, an area of

Frontierland, a piece of Liberty Square. But much of this was foreign to him—parts of a park never before seen.

"Come look!" Wayne said, now standing by the small window. He tore the theatrical gel from the window.

The kids joined him, squeezing together.

Below, the dark park filled with light, following the same pattern that the ink flowed through the plans. Light rushed up lanes and streets, jumped over benches and engorged trees. Attractions came alive. First on the outer edge of the Magic Kingdom, but steadily rushing toward the castle.

Faster and faster the light traveled through the park, brighter and brighter. It arrived at the castle from all directions, a brilliant white light racing up the walls. The kids jumped back, blinded.

The sky erupted with fireworks, throwing blazing color and light into the heavens, deafening explosions and blinding colors.

The local newspapers would report the next day that a private party at the Magic Kingdom had been responsible for the most amazing show of fireworks the park had ever seen. But Finn and the other DHIs would know differently.

With the sky still erupting outside, Wayne walked

over to Finn and extended a hand of thanks. They shook hands. The kids cheered and formed a huddle. As they spun in celebration, Wayne returned to the coffee table. There, he picked up the black remote.

And pushed the button.